BEHIND THE
FLYING SAUCER
MYSTERY

(original title: Flying Saucers Farewell)

George Adamski

PAPERBACK LIBRARY, INC.

NEW YORK

I dedicate this book to a better understanding of our place in the Universe.

—George Adamski

FOREWORD

THE PURPOSE of this book is to share with my many friends throughout the world knowledge gained through personal experiences during the years since *Inside the Space Ships** was published in 1955.

I wish to express deep appreciation to my devoted colleagues and friends—from this world and other planets—who have assisted me in preparing the material contained herein.

George Adamski

INTRODUCTION

FOR THIRTEEN YEARS I have pursued the elusive "flying saucers," investigating every available fact in an attempt to solve the many questions created by their presence.

Now many of the riddles have been solved on the basis of scientific proof, and I am firmly convinced that men from other planets have arrived on Earth!

In this conviction I am not alone. Many scientists and government officials now admit their belief that people from other planets in our solar system have come to Earth and that flying saucers are spacecraft of extra-terrestrial origin.

In 1957 I first met George Adamski, space lecturer-philosopher who, with the British writer Desmond Leslie, co-authored *Flying Saucers Have Landed,* one of the most informative documents to be published on spacecraft and their origin. Adamski's startling account of his meeting with a man from Venus met with tremendous response from readers throughout the world. Since my first meeting with George Adamski, we have worked together on an extensive study of what some officials prefer to call "Unidentified Flying Objects."

My interest in UFO's actually began many years ago in Boise, Idaho, where I lived at the time of Kenneth Arnold's first report in 1947.

In those days I worked as a radio repairman for an auto electric shop and had serviced the radios in Arnold's private plane and automobile. Arnold visited the shop shortly after the Mount Rainier incident, when he sighted a formation of UFO's, and I was very impressed with his story. I knew Arnold to be a sober individual and had no reason to doubt his experience.

I maintained this interest for several years afterward. In the summer of 1951, I moved to Seattle, Washington, where I read occasional UFO reports in the newspapers, most of them tongue-in-cheek accounts which hinted that hallucinations, or perhaps crackpots, might be behind the flying saucer stories.

Then I bought a pocket book entitled *Flying Saucers Are Real,* by Donald E. Keyhoe. This book convinced me that saucers were indeed real and were of interplanetary origin. I began to purchase every UFO book I could get my hands on, as fast as it was released to the public.

All contact claims I dismissed as pure fantasy, written by willful hoaxers or by sincere though deluded people.

One morning I read an advertisement in the Seattle *Post-Intelligencer* requesting that persons interested in UFO's contact Robert J. Gribble of the Civilian Flying Saucer Intelligence. (This group later changed its name to Aerial Phenomena Research Group.) I contacted Gribble and joined his organization. A few months later, Gribble invited me to become an associate director in the group and to participate more actively in its UFO research program. This I did and got in on the ground floor, so to speak, of what I consider to be the best and most scientific investigation agency in the UFO field.

Each month clippings would pour in from every major newspaper in the world. Gribble maintained large maps pinpointing all the major sightings and landings in the world. Separate maps were used for other incidents connected with the UFO's.

In July of 1957 I moved to Southern California. At this time a new opportunity presented itself; I was very close to the majority of the so-called contactees.

Some months previously I had come to the realization that contacts of some kind must have been made. If the situation were reversed and our ships were flying around another planet for several years, they would certainly in that length of time try to land and contact some of the natives. If we landed and accidentally ran across an inhabitant, no matter what his station in life might be, we would certainly attempt some sort of communication. The space people would be no different from us in that respect.

As a result of all this, I decided I'd better pull my head out of the sand and investigate the contactee claimants. I drove hundreds of miles on weekends and visited many people. All of them were fine, friendly persons but I was very disappointed; not one had proof of any kind. Many were establishing cults, with one in California even incorporating as a "religion." None of these people were genuine. Some freely stated their experiences were not physical, but occurred as "psychic" or "astral" contacts. Several claimed contact via Ouija boards, automatic handwriting, trances, or equally ridiculous methods. None of them seemed to realize these incidents were products of their own wishful thinking and meant absolutely nothing to anyone but themselves.

At this point I was so disgusted with the whole flying saucer business I didn't even bother to visit George Adamski. I assumed he was just like the rest.

A few months later my family and I traveled to Mount Palomar to see the 200-inch Hale Telescope. After an enjoyable day on top, we were returning down the mountain when I noticed Adamski's name on a mailbox. I decided to stop, as I was preparing a series of lectures on flying saucers and I didn't want to talk against someone I had never met. I was determined to expose the whole contactee setup as a hoax.

Imagine my surprise when I met a man who appeared to be as distinguished as a college professor and who talked of scientific things as an expert; who claimed his contacts were real and physical and further stated that contacts were in no way connected with so-called "mystic phenomena," "psychism" or "spiritualism."

Adamski produced clear photographs and affidavits from many witnesses who were present when the photos were taken and the contact established. No one else had ever done this. At last I was getting somewhere, proceeding on a sane, logical course.

In Adamski's 16-mm. color motion picture, the large metalic dome of a spacecraft was clearly visible. Expert photographers had examined his pictures and stated they couldn't even be faked with expensive "motion picture studio" equipment. Orthographic projections comparing Adamski's films with pictures taken overseas proved that models were not used. Each fact served to cinch the authenticity a little tighter.

I became intrigued enough to revisit Adamski, and on a few occasions I met scientists and military technicians who had come for information to be used in their research laboratories. These men took Adamski at face value and I began to gain increased respect for him.

I compiled all the information I received about Adamski and of the material he furnished to the research laboratories. Later I read newspaper accounts of how the re-entry heating problem of our missiles had been solved. The method was the same as outlined by Adamski several months previously.

I read letters from scientists thanking Adamski for his information and stating the methods he outlined had worked.

When the now notorious "Straith Letter" arrived from the U.S. State Department, I participated in the two-month investigation that followed. Much of the information that arrived concerning the Straith Letter has never been made public, and so I leave it to Adamski to release or hold as he sees fit. The facts boiled down to one thing, though. The "Straith Letter" was never disproved! The same cover-up was attempted with the letter as with the UFO itself. Before long I was actively working with Adamski in his effort to "tell the American public what it should know," as the "Straith Letter" had asked.

During the latter part of 1958, I traveled with Adamski on a 4,000-mile lecture tour reaching as far north as Bellingham, Washington. During the intermission of our lecture in Everett, Washington, a public information officer from Paine Air Force Base came up to us and complimented Adamski on his scientific, down-to-earth and physical approach to the subject. He stated that when the psychics were kicked out of the UFO situation, the Air Force would be able to release its information. He said the mystics had so confused the issue with their false claims of contact that the general public looked with ridicule at the whole matter and refused to accept any of it.

After all, what normal, intelligent person would be seen at a "séance" attended by persons who claimed they left their bodies behind at night and flew off into the wild blue yonder to ride in a space ship? The average person would never accept a fantastic claim that "astral entities" and spirits were

11

flying around in invisible ships, materializing and dematerializing at will.

Notice how, overnight, the mediums abandoned their Indian guides and substituted "spacemen."

As a result of my investigation, I whole-heartedly back George Adamski and the other legitimate, though mostly unknown, contactees. So far, Adamski is the only well-known contactee claimant in the United States who has proven legitimate.

His photos are the only publicly-known pictures to be listed as authentic by the intelligence agencies of many world governments. In the files of certain governments, his name heads the list of authentic contactees. His photos are used universally to illustrate the true appearance of a flying saucer.

At one time he was asked to undergo a government security check and lecture at military installations around the world. This he refused to do, since such an arrangement would have bound him to secrecy, closing his information to the public.

During Adamski's world tour in 1959, certain heads of governments informed him they were also contactees. It is evident the space visitors have not confined their visits to the United States.

In regard to knowledge about the space people and their reasons for coming, the United States falls sadly behind the majority of other nations. Perhaps Americans will soon realize that a vast new horizon has opened before us, a limitless destiny which only the open, alert mind will inherit.

Now, let us hear of that destiny from George Adamski, who, I sincerely believe, was one of the first Americans to meet the people from other planets.

C. A. Honey
Anaheim, California
July, 1960

BOOK I

1. WHY THEY CAME

IT WAS IN OCTOBER, 1946, that the U.S.A. shot its first radar beam to the moon. This was for experimental purposes. The center of the moon was the target, since our scientists thought they had accurate calculations of the distances between our planet and her satellite. The intent was to learn the time required for a radar signal to travel such a distance through outer space and return.

At that time considerable publicity was given to the feat and its achievement, but, so far as the public has been informed, the matter was dropped there. Yet, in reality, that event was only the beginning of our rapid progress spaceward.

According to the spacepeople with whom I have had the pleasure of discussing the subject, the radar signal sent out at that time hit the edge of the moon and ricocheted into space, alerting watchers at their instruments on Mars and Venus. Its strangeness was mistakenly interpreted to be a signal of distress. Immediately they answered with their own signals. When no replies were received, their ships were dispatched to investigate. Naturally these went to the section of our planet whence the signals had originated.

This explains why, in the beginning, more spacecraft were observed over the U.S.A. than other parts of the world. And, as it will be when our space ships reach other planets, some of their craft landed here and there as they found it safe or necessary. Because they were unfamiliar with our terrain and atmosphere (we had been experimenting with atomic bombs and, not long before, had exploded some to end the war, thereby setting up an unnatural condition), or the strength of our planet's magnetic fields, there were more crashes than we realize. Frank Scully reported some of these in 1950 in his book *Behind the Flying Saucers*.* If a person happened to be in the vicinity of a landed craft, the crewmen inevitably

*Henry Holt and Co., New York.

endeavored to meet and talk with him. When successful, they always explained why they had been attracted to Earth in increased numbers.

Our space travelers will do the same, I am sure. It is only natural!

It was this information that enabled me to tell whether a claimed contactee was telling the truth, or indulging in wishful thinking, because one having an actual experience of this kind would mention this part of the conversation during his relating of his meeting with people from a space ship. I have never divulged this fact previously because it would have served as a basis upon which imposters could work. Now, however, I have been given a means of identification, and the Brothers have suggested that this information be made public at this time in order to answer many questions heretofore unanswered.

In 1946, shortly after the echo of our signal had returned to Earth from the moon, our scientists began picking up strange code signals which they were unable to understand. Time calculations indicated that these signals were coming from our neighboring planets, in spite of accepted scientific theories that for many reasons human life was impossible there. Other signals seemed to be coming from open space, an unexplainable and unbelievable state of affairs, unless one took space vehicles into consideration.

Not only did these signals continue for several months, they are still being received!

Our scientists have worked diligently in an effort to decode them . . . at first, without success. Their accomplishments through the years have naturally been kept secret from the general public. Nonetheless, today in America we have Project OZMA at the Green Bank Radio Observatory in West Virginia; England has her gigantic Jodrell Bank radio telescope; Australia has her Mills Cross, along with other radio telescopes and is now in the process of building a 210-foot circular radio telescope scheduled to be completed in April, 1961. This will be the largest in the Southern Hemisphere, but I am sure there are many others throughout the world, all delicately tuned and receiving signals from space which the scientists are endeavoring to decipher.

Our Bible contains several hundred reports of space visitations, as of which have been misinterpreted and misunderstood until recent years, due to the many translations as well as personal interpretations and teachings of Biblical records. Today many researchers are conceding that the history of our earth and its inhabitants was old when our Bible history began. It was prior to that time that interplanetary communication was normal between our planet and her neighbors. Most of our early records have been lost and our education since has not admitted the possibility of anything of this kind. Yet, regardless of our understanding or lack of it, spacecraft have moved through our atmosphere now and then through the centuries.

Many sightings of these craft have been recorded during the centuries, both by scientists and by the man on the street. But because even yet we have not entirely outgrown our fears of the unknown, and certain witchcraft ideas, reports of these sightings have, for the most part, remained in closed files, forgotten because of fear of ridicule and persecution of those having such experiences.

Desmond Leslie of London, England, spent years and endless effort in compiling many of these records. The results of his efforts were published in 1953 in *Flying Saucers Have Landed,** in which my report of having met a man from Venus was also included.

Visits from spacecraft to our earth during the past several centuries might be compared to ocean-liner visits to some far out-of-the-way island which is visited perhaps once or twice a year to leave supplies and pick up merchandise of the natives. Occasionally some of their people would wish to remain on Earth to become better acquainted with our people and their ways. A certain percentage of these have liked it here and have remained. Others have returned home after certain lengths of time. In this way the people of our neighboring planets have been able to keep in touch with some conditions on earth. This practice continues today, with many governments having records of identification for these interplanetary visitors.

*British Book Centre, Inc., New York.

In 1946, when our signal was first picked up and their ships were alerted with instructions to investigate, an increase in numbers of spacecraft moving through Earth's atmosphere took place. For the following twelve years this increase was continued, with sightings reported over every nation in the world. Official documentary records can be found in the files of practically every nation as the elusive objects have been picked up on radar screens in the U.S.A., England, Russia, Brazil, New Zealand, Australia, and many others, often over their capital cities as well as above their research laboratories, their testing grounds, moving with and around their missiles as if studying them closely, and at times moving in close proximity to airplanes and ships.

Many books have been written which include sightings in large numbers, or singly by individuals alone, or at times in the sight of hundreds of witnesses, as in 1954 in Bilbao, Spain, when a formation of flying saucers flew slowly and at quite low altitude above the multitude so they could be seen easily without binoculars. In this incident, according to a newspaper report, a portion of the citizens knelt.

Rome, too, has had her visits from formations of spacecraft moving overhead, watched by people in the streets. At the time, these were mistakenly taken for Russian squadrons on reconnaissance flights, but there were those who knew better, and later these events were publicized for what they actually were.

In Mexico in 1952, in the dark of night, a passenger train was escorted by a flying saucer for more than an hour. Sometimes this craft moved above the train, or it would move ahead and wait for long moments. The glow from this aerial ship was so bright that the passengers were able to see one another, or to read as if in full daylight. Testimony of this event was taken from all the passengers, the crewmembers, and some technicians who were traveling on the train. These were documented and notarized, and I have been told that these records are in the hands of competent Mexican authorities.

Several years ago during "Exercise Ardent" in England, the radar station picked up images of ten ships that flew from England to Holland above the British air forces. Their speed was estimated to be above 30,000 kilometers per hour, according to the report. They suddenly disappeared from the radar screen.

From Australia, during the latter part of 1959 and the first half of 1960, detailed published reports were shared with the world about Father Gill, a priest who, with a number of his parishioners and a fellow-clergyman, watched a large spacecraft hover not too far above them in their little town in New Guinea, while repairs were being made on the craft. This lasted for a considerable time, and was repeated a few days later. Father Gill traveled through Australia, giving public lectures on the event. He also talked over radio and TV in order to reach as many people as possible with the story of his experiences.

During the summer of 1959 an air show was being held in Canada. Thousands of people attended. During the height of the show a large Russian jet came in, and behind it but staying a short distance above as the jet landed, was an immense space ship. According to reports brought to me by several who were there and saw it, portholes along the sides of the gigantic cigar-shaped ship were open and people looked at the multitudes on the ground, as they in turn observed those in the ship. Those in the ship were described to me as men, women, and children, judged from their appearances, differing in color as Earth's people. Changes were made in the faces at the portholes as those having a look moved away to give room to others. Some of the children looked so small it was thought they had to be lifted up to see out, the same as we do with our children.

Naturally I asked my informants, who had driven hundreds of miles to tell me of their experiences, why someone had not taken pictures of both the Russian jet and the spacecraft as they flew in and came to a standstill. The spacecraft remained hovering for several minutes before turning its nose upward and disappearing from sight at a fantastic speed, according to the report. The reply was that, of course, hundreds of people present with cameras had taken pictures, but after the space ship had moved away, the Canadian military had moved in and confiscated the film in every camera.

I was told later that the report of this event went over the press wires at the time, but with instructions to kill it and not let it be published.

Through the years Brazil has had her share of sightings and personal contacts with space visitors. Some of these have been publicized in Brazilian papers, but few have been able to get beyond. Now, I am told, Brazil is making an effort to get other nations to acknowledge the reality of our space visitors, open their "secret" files on the subject to the people of the world, and make an attempt to be more friendly with these space neighbors in order to learn more from them that the entire world might benefit from their knowledge and their presence.

It is a well-known fact that although, for reasons best known to themselves, government officials throughout the world have persistently refused to admit the reality of spacecraft moving through our atmosphere, they do admit the presence of Unidentified Flying Objects. From time to time they endeavor to excuse or explain these things as "nothing," due to their own inability to locate the craft upon investigation, perhaps several hours, days or weeks later. But obviously this is merely to pacify the general public, who would be much happier with the truth contained in government files. This consists of authenticated records and photographs, many of which were taken by their own personnel and aircraft.

Through the centuries, crewmen of space ships have taken samples of our earth, plants, water, etc. for analysis. In this way they have been able to keep informed of changes taking place on the surface of our planet, and in its minerals. And as I told in my book *Inside the Space Ships,** they have taken frequent samples of our atmosphere, especially since our scientists have been experimenting with atomic explosions. Now their researches are becoming more detailed than they have been for thousands of years, because they have become actively interested in us and our planet, and more of their ships have come our way. They know that our planet is undergoing a natural, periodic change which will have its

*published as *Inside the Flying Saucers* by Paperback Library, Inc. (# 53-428, 60¢)

effect upon outer space, and in turn upon their planets in varying degrees.

When our ships reach the moon and our neighboring planets, the crewmen will likewise bring back samples of their earth, plants, water, etc., for scientific analysis and comparison with ours, I'm sure.

If it were not for these space ships moving through our atmosphere in such numbers that they could no longer be denied and discredited by our researchers, and if it were not for the help given Earth's scientists of all nations, both personally and by mental impressions when a researcher's mind was open for inspiration, our space program would not have progressed as it has. Although they have not been able to give us their full knowledge, our friends from space have shared with us as much as we were able to accept. As with all nature, growth and progress is slow; so we must grow in respect and understanding of the powers with which we are working before we can successfully harness and use them beneficially. Our scientists are doing just this, and within a matter of a few years, we will be joining our neighbors in interplanetary flight in our own Earth-made ships, if we are wise and forego further destructive wars that may well annihilate Mankind from the face of this Earth.

Our neighbors on other planets had to go through the growing stage, just as our scientists have, except they have not had the setbacks we have experienced through a history of wars and destruction. They too were helped by those who had learned the answers to space travel. On Venus, Mars, and some of the other planets in our system, scientists studied deeply the secrets of Nature, her actions and reactions, with satisfactory results. Thus, with the help of other space travelers and inspiration from Nature, they succeeded centuries ago in accomplishing that which today we are endeavoring to do.

Strange as it may seem to us who have been taught our present system of mathematics, Nature works on the principle of one and one adding up to three. The positive and negative, brought together in relationship, result in an effect . . . the third part of the equation, the offspring, in which a certain percentage of the original two primal forces has been maintained. In other words, the offspring has the benefits of its parents within itself. Were it not for the operation of this Law, there would be no food to eat, nor continuance of life of any kind.

The Law too was known and used on Earth centuries ago, but somewhere the zero was injected into our mathematics. Nowhere in Nature can inactivity or a state of nothingness exist, as represented by the zero. Thus there is no 10, 20, etc. in Natural Law.

The Cosmic principle of mathematics takes us from one to nine, but does not go into numbers, plus nothing. Instead, it progresses from nine, to nine plus one, which might be expressed as 9.1. Upon reaching nine plus nine, 9.9, the count proceeds to a multiple factor of nine: 18. From there it progresses to 18.1, and so on until 18.9 again becomes a multiple of nine, making 27. And so on without end.

Because of our introduction of zero, or "nothing," into our mathematical systems, it may take many years before we learn to think in Cosmic mathematical terms.

In *Behind the Flying Saucers*,* Frank Scully mentioned that in the first crashed spacecraft examined by our scientists some twelve to fifteen years ago, all measurements were found to be divisible by nine. Thus he gave the first clue to Cosmic mathematics used in construction of the spacecraft.

Although one of the first books written on this subject of spacecraft, and bitterly denied by the opposition who feared the acceptance of such facts even in those days, this book stands as one that has never been disproved. Of the hundreds of books written regarding space visitors and their ships, this remains one of the comparatively few authentic treatments of the subject.

Built in compliance with Cosmic principle, these ships operate on Cosmic forces. We have much yet to learn about these forces, but our scientists are researching constantly in an effort to gain this understanding.

Study of the atom is their first effort. They have learned much, both of its dangers and the potential for constructive uses of the atom. Atomic blasts such as we have developed

*Henry Holt and Co., New York.

are destructive in a terrible way. Why, when the atom is considered to be the building-block of all forms? In Nature atoms blend with others for which they have an affinity and harmony results. But in our scientifiic efforts we have divided natural atomic combinations and have forced together elements that have no affinity for one another. Negatives or positives, denied their natural opposites, exert all their power to part company and seek those opposites. Confined under pressure, when proper conditions are set up, an explosion results with disastrous effects both from the force of the explosion and the unbalanced released atoms seeking to balance themselves.

To date, our scientists in their atomic research have found a use for certain elements, while at the same time establishing vast stockpiles of other elements whose accumulation results in lethal conditions. Since they have so far found no use for this waste, they seal it into huge lead drums and drop them into the sea. But this is not the correct solution to the problem. These pressured elements will continue exerting their energy toward escape, and in time will free themselves to join with other elements for which they have an affinity. The result will be disastrous to life of all variety.

On the other hand, scientists on other planets have found means of using the elements which we throw away, by allowing them to unite in certain proportions with other elements, by which they obtain usable energy. In this way they maintain the natural balance of their planets.

It may seem difficult for some to understand why people who have progressed so far ahead of us intellectually should continue having accidents. But one must remember that there is always an unknown factor to be taken into consideration. The minerals on their planets are like those on Earth. Scientists, manufacturers, mechanics on Earth who study and work with metals of all kinds, know that conditions sometimes arise in which metals do not react as expected. It has not been too many years that we have been reading about "tired" metal. Natural conditions set up a variety of effects, many of which can be anticipated, others of which cannot. Even Nature herself has a habit of performing in unexpected ways, especially when interfered with by the efforts of men.

Man too is an unpredictable product of Nature. Thus the effects of his efforts, even when working with other products of Nature, will inevitably be subject to faults of one kind or another which may result in minor or major accidents.

The wise man learns from all such experiences and through continuous effort progresses along the pathway of life, wherever he may be living.

With so many of their ships moving through our atmosphere, permitting close observation of Earth's people and their ways, it did not take long for the space travelers to learn of the many divisions and misunderstandings existing in our world. Their history showed the fallacy of such conditions, and the inevitable results such as we are experiencing today. The Cosmic plan is for a united people on each planet.

Although their original purpose in coming was to answer what they thought was a signal for help from us, and to alert us if necessary to natural changes taking place in our solar system, they also turned their efforts toward helping us broaden our concepts of human relations, that we might halt our head-long race toward nuclear destruction.

From this closer association with Earthlings, they were surprised to find how really little accurate understanding we had of ourselves, let alone of the atmosphere surrounding our planet—practically nothing of the ionosphere, our protective electromagnetic shield, and its purpose—with no true knowledge whatever of the Cosmos of which we are a part.

They sent increasing numbers of their ships, both large and small, to cruise through our atmosphere in the hope that people's curiosity would be stimulated toward seeking greater understanding of what was taking place, and of the ownership of these strange craft. More and more of their people landed to live among us in the hope that, through their presence, we would be influenced by their kindness, their lack of criticism of others, and their willingness to be friends with all. Furthermore, through casual conversations they could awaken sleeping minds to a vaster concept of life and the Cosmos.

Even then they did not realize for awhile the many fears that the presence of their ships in our skies would create. Nor were they able to conceive the depth to which such fears

22

would incite us: that official orders would be issued for them to be shot down. As a result, some of their ships were destroyed and the crewmen killed.

In spite of their understanding of life and its continuance, they did not appreciate such acts on our part. It did not take them long to learn to stay beyond the range of our ships and their attack abilities, although coming near enough for close observation through their technical instruments. They were also able at times to increase the repulsive power within their force fields, thus repelling the smaller of our bullets. In this way they lessened the danger to themselves, while still being able to continue the work for which they came.

2. SPACE ACTIVITY WITHIN OUR SOLAR SYSTEM

ONE OF THE most frequent problems encountered when giving a lecture on space is the insistence of scientists that the outer planets are devoid of light and heat. Their objection is that radiation from the sun is so weak at these vast distances that Pluto, for instance, would be at absolute zero or close to it, with a frozen atmosphere, and totally incapable of supporting life-forms of any type.

This is the main argument brought against me when doubt is expressed about my meeting human beings from some of these other planets.

The first thing to realize is that the sun does not emit light and heat in the form we observe here on Earth. Radiation from the sun does not manifest itself as light and heat until it penetrates the atmospheres of the planets themselves. Outer space is devoid of light as we know it. The light in outer space is a cold light caused by the phosphorescence of vast clouds of particles and gases responding to the radiation given off by the sun. To a human observer, outer space looks like a dark, vast void, filled with billions upon billions of tiny specks of multicolored light. All of these tiny lights are in a state of continuous motion and activity.

Radiation from the sun is composed of ultra-violet light, hard and soft X-rays, cosmic and gamma rays. The greater portion of these destructive rays are filtered out by a planet's ionosphere and upper atmosphere. The innumerable, infinitesimal particles within a planet's atmosphere emit visible light when excited by the sun's filtered radiation. The earth absorbs these rays, and in return gives off infra-red energy. Energy thus given off activates the atmosphere immediately surrounding the planet, thereby generating heat that keeps the planet warm.

It is easy to see how this energy from the sun can encompass our earth. After all, we are only 93 million miles from the sun. But what about the planets that are more remote from the sun?

According to standard textbooks, the radiation from the sun decreases inversely with the square of the distance. In layman's language, this means that if you double the distance from the sun, the radiation would be only one-fourth as great. If you double the distance again, the radiation would be only one-sixteenth as great, and so on. If the sun's radiation actually decreases at this rate, then the outer planets must indeed be in a state of perpetual coldness.

What, then, is the answer? I know from personal experience that these outer planets have thriving civilizations, with climates and atmospheres similar to our own earth. The larger planets, such as Saturn and Jupiter, have much lower gravity than has been assumed by our sicentists. Therefore, our explanation of gravity must be in error in some way.

Our main problem now is not gravity but climate. How do these planets receive enough energy from the sun to exist in a similar state to Earth?

A clue to this answer is found in the vacuum tube; more specifically it is found in the cathode ray tube. This tube, abbreviated CRT, is found in the ordinary home television receiver. In it we have a heater that raises the temperature of a cathode to a point at which it gives off electrons in great quantities. These electrons are negative in nature. High positive voltages are supplied to various grids and anodes in the tube.

There are two types of electricity: positive and negative. The electron is negative and its counterpart, the proton, is positive. Just as the north pole of a magnet will attract the south pole of another magnet, the electrons attract the pro-

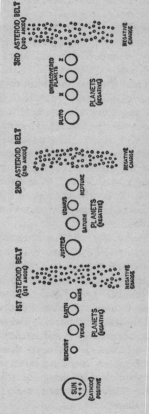

CATHODE RAY TUBE

OUR SOLAR SYSTEM

25

tons. Similar poles of magnets repel each other and so do similar charges of electricity. Likes repel; unlikes attract.

The high positive voltages on the grids and anodes of the CRT attract the electrons from the cathode. The electrons are pulled toward the anodes with great speed, but, due to the type of construction of these anodes, most electrons rush right on through toward the next one. Theoretically, this could be continued for great distances by use of several different anodes and high positive voltages.

Mercury, Venus, Earth and Mars are close enough to the sun to get good radiation. With the planets beyond Mars it is a different situation. At these distances the sun's radiation has started to diminish. At this time it comes under the influence of the tremendous attracting force generated by the first asteroid belt which totally envelops the central portion of our solar system. The negative charge of the asteroid belt is great enough to attract the particles from the sun and pull them back up to their original speed. Because this belt is grid-like in construction, with thousands of openings and paths, similar to a window screen with air going through, the particles dash on through and enter the influence of the planets beyond.

These, being negative in themselves, as are all planets, attract from space the positive particles they need for light and heat. At the same time infinite numbers of similar particles rush on past and are attracted by a second asteroid belt between Neptune and Pluto, where the process is repeated all over again. This furnishes Pluto and the last three planets with normal light and heat. (Twelve planets in all exist in our system, according to the space travelers.)

A third asteroid belt is beyond the twelfth planet, serving a dual purpose of blending space within our system with that of neighboring systems. At the same time it serves as a protective filter, comparable to the ionosphere encompassing a planet.

We might summarize by saying: The two inner asteroid belts gather rays from the sun and speed them on through space. They equalize, so to speak, conditions within the system from the area of Mercury right on to the outer reaches of our solar system, while the third keeps our system, as a unit, in balance with those beyond. Because of this cosmic activity, of which we on Earth have not previously been aware, we could go to any of our planets and enjoy a climate and atmosphere similar to our own.

With the asteroid belt, basically negative in nature, attracting sun rays varying in length, speed, width, and charge, a condition is set into action comparable to an alternating current in electricity. Some of the positive particles are trapped within the asteroid belt, while others zip right on through to radiate through space beyond. The law of attraction and repulsion permits a state of cohesion to take place between some of the particles within the belt, building larger forms, while a major percentage remain in their natural state. Particles of many sizes thus created are caused to constantly act upon one another in energy and matter alike. This very action, while building some forms, also disintegrates other forms by separating the particles of which they are composed.

Serving at Nature's dielectric in this manner, the asteroid belt, I have been told, is the womb of the Cosmos out of which planets are born. When a planet reaches its peak of service in a system and starts on the path of decline and disintegration, a body is drawn from the asteroid belt by the magnetic influence of that planet's orbit to maintain the perfect balance of the system. So, as the old planet disintegrates, a new one is built to replace it. On a larger scale, systems go through the same cycle of birth, growth and extinction and follow the pattern as do all forms in Nature.

In using the term "extinction," I am referring to matter going back into the gaseous or invisible state. It is not destroyed; it is only changed in form. A good example of this is seen when ice becomes water and finally evaporates into vapor.

After matter has returned to its original or gaseous state, it is free to start the cycle all over again. It may travel across interplanetary distances and become part of another planet or it may return to become a part of its original planet, serving in the construction of new forms.

With this continuous interchange between the planets, it is only natural to find each planet has similar materials in its make-up and similar plant and animal life on its surface . . . with a few exceptions.

27

Billions of giant Milky-Way systems or galaxies, like our own, are known to exist throughout the vast reaches of the never-ending Cosmos. Toward the center of these giant systems so far observed by our telescopes are found the newer and hotter stars. As the galaxy expands outward, these stars cool and planetary systems are born.

In these cooler outer edges are billions of life-supporting planets. Here also are vast clouds of oxygen and hydrogen spreading out over thousands of light years of distance. This is readily apparent from examination of recent color photographs taken with the 200-inch telescope at Mount Palomar. Made with a newly developed super-color film, these photographs show great bluish clouds of oxygen, and the reddish clouds of hydrogen existing throughout about 65 per cent of most observable galaxies. The only area where these gases are not apparent is in the hot nucleus of the galaxy itself.

In our own Solar System our sun is only one of a group of some 100,000 million stars. Several hundred thousand inhabited planets could easily be in existence in our Milky Way Solar System alone.

Imagine if you can this pattern of suns and their associated planets multiplied billions of times, extending without beginning or end!

Man and his ego has said that our earth is the center of this vast array. He has refused to consider the possibility of our planet not being unique in the Cosmos. Now he is being forcibly awakened . . . first by friendly visits from our neighbors, whose interplanetary ships have been seen moving through our atmosphere and over every nation in our world, and now by our own space explorations.

All of these wonders are awaiting us as we slowly measure our way step by step into outer space, of which we know so little. Already many ancient but accepted theories have been cast aside. As the Cosmos lies before us, understanding extends unlimited to the seeking mind, as did new lands to our pioneers of old. There were the pioneers of Earth. Today we are pioneers of space with its ceaseless activity and endless wonders . . . worlds upon worlds . . . expressions of the one Infinite Creator.

3. SPACE SHIPS AND GRAVITY

As the earthman plans voyages into outer space, he is faced to a certain degree with problems comparable in many ways to those of the ancient mariner, for throughout space there are definite natural lanes, just as the oceans have their currents. Our pilots have found "rivers in space" above our planet as they were flying at certain altitudes. These were located by chance, but since have been described in numerous articles published in aviation magazines. Our scientists and our airmen are aware of various types of currents moving through the atmosphere, comparable to those of the oceans. We will find similar conditions throughout all space, between planets and systems.

As they studied such conditions in the atmospheres encompassing their own planets, inhabitants of other worlds were able to develop their first ships enabling them to venture into outer space. Since that time space has become as safe and simple for them to travel as the atmosphere through which our planes fly from place to place on Earth. They quickly realized that if they were to go out and return safely home, they could not burden their ships with heavy loads of fuel, but would have to learn how to use Nature's energy for their propulsion power. So it was along these lines that their scientists worked, and finally succeeded.

To understand more clearly the magnetic propulsion of interplanetary spacecraft, we must first consider geomagnetism, the magnetic sphere of influence which surrounds every planet and every sun, filling all space.

We can liken Earth's geomagnetic field to the series of circular ripples created by dropping a pebble into a pond. These circular ripples move outward from the center point where the pebble was dropped; expanding in size, but diminishing in force as they move.

If we simultaneously drop two pebbles into the pond, several feet apart, two sets of expanding circular waves are created, moving outward from each central point. Where the wave fronts meet, an interference pattern is formed which extends between the two center points.

This interference pattern assumes the shape of an extended ellipse, with its smaller ends at the points where the pebbles were dropped. Although both wave fronts have diminished in force as they traveled outward from their central points, the interference pattern has combined a portion of both forces to create a third force, which remains constant between the two central points so long as they remain active.

The same relationship exists between the expanding spheres of magnetic influence which move into space from the sun, and from each planet or satellite. As these magnetic wave fronts expand from another source, they form a magnetic interference pattern which again assumes the general shape of an extended ellipse. Although the geomagnetic field of each planet or sun diminishes in strength as it moves spaceward, the elliptical magnetic fields thus created between celestial bodies by magnetic interferences maintain a constant-strength magnetic field between the bodies.

A planet's magnetic field is similar to "direct current," which grows weaker as it travels from its source; however, the elliptical magnetic field shared by two planets may be likened to "alternating current," which can be transmitted over long distances.

These alternating elliptical fields, extending from sun to planet, and from planet to planet, are the invisible bonds which balance the Solar System. They extend in similar fashion between systems, and between galaxies. They also exist between the micro-magnetic fields of atoms, the "miniature solar systems."

The "end zones" of elliptical fields which influence Earth extend from about 58 degrees north latitude to 58 degrees south latitude. The axis of each elliptical field is at right angles to the magnetic polar axis, and the elliptical field axis corresponds to Earth's magnetic equator.

The "magnetic rivers" between planets constantly alternate or change their direction of flow, creating a two-way magnetic pulse between planets. By using only one half of each two-way pulse, space liners move in one direction. For example, if the spacecraft uses only an outward pulse, it moves away from a planet. If the ship uses an inward pulse, it moves toward a planet. If the spacecraft allows the alternating pulse to flow through it in both directions, it can hover.

To explain how the space ships operate within a planet's gravitational field, we must first recognize the relationship between goemagnetism and the planet's rotation.

On Earth many writers have referred to "anti-gravity" devices, and in our scientific researches the idea has been introduced that gravity can be wrestled to a standstill. This is not an efficient approach.

Space ships that today are visiting our world from other planets operate on a "pro-gravitic" principle, using the natural forces, instead of attempting to fight them. Since these ships operate on electrostatic power, it would be useless for them to fight the geomagntic forces, since Earth's geomagnetic field alone has an electrical potential of billions of volts.

Planetary gravity is the natural balance between the centrifugal force of a planet's axial velocity and the centripetal attraction of its electrostatic field. Centrifugal force tries to spin an object from the planet's surface, but electrostatic attraction keeps the object from flying into space.

If electrostatic attraction did not exist, we would have to hang firmly to a tree or rock to keep from being hurled into space by centrifugal force. By the same token, if centrifugal force did not exist to balance electrostatic attraction and its inward centripetal force, we would be flattened against the earth's surface.

I believe the late Dr. Albert Einstein described this balanced, inseparable relationship in his Unified Field Theory; however, my observations are not so profound as those achieved by that great abstract scientist.

We have briefly challenged the gravitational force with our aircraft and rockets. Now it is time to consider the benefits we can derive from putting that force to work for us.

A rocket is pushed forward by a concentrated chemical thrust that is greater than the pull of gravity. The "ionic rockets" we are now planning will expel ions out of their engines and achieve thrust exactly like the chemical rockets. Ionic rockets, however, can not operate efficiently within the unified field of a planet. They are only efficient in the near-vacuum of outer space.

31

A flying saucer, or "pro-gravitic" craft, operates by generating its own gravitational field, which surrounds it in a generally spherical pattern. This field is adjusted to resonate, or blend in harmony with the planet's geomagnetic field. The resonating gravitational field causes the ship to be weightless. In this weightless or balanced condition, the ship, wherever it may be, can be moved by a relatively slight thrust.

Our ionic rockets are designed to exert the electrical thrust of ionized particles, a thrust so relatively small it has been termed slight as "a butterfly's sigh." In outer space, however, where the ionic rocket would be "weightless," because it would be free of planetary gravity, this tiny "sigh" of ionic power could propel the rocket at speeds eventually reaching three million miles per hour, according to present theory.

Within its self-generated pro-gravitic field, the saucer can travel at a rate exceeding the speed of light! Using the forces of Nature, its movement can be the same as that of natural forces. The propelling power as produced by the generator within the spacecraft can be compared to that provided by the Van de Graaff electrostatic generators which are used in our own physics laboratories.

An interesting laboratory demonstration which simulates the effect of a hovering saucer can be achieved by placing an aluminum ring over the vertical core of a large electromagnet. By passing an alternating current through the electromagnet, controlled with a rheostat, the aluminum ring can be made to hover. The saucers, however, generate their own resonating fields, instead of "floating" on magnetic eddy currents as in the case of the aluminum ring.

Electrostatic thrust can be demonstrated by placing a tiny strip of aluminum foil near the discharge globe of a Van de Graaff generator. The foil will orbit the discharge globe, with no mechanical connection!

Saucers have often been described as "glowing." Such a condition is created when natural particles in space, through which a ship is moving, come into contact with its encompassing field of resonant frequency. Pulsations within this field cause a shimmering effect, like heat waves rising from pavement, which makes the craft appear to be "alive and breathing." This effort can also bend the light waves entirely around the craft, causing it to suddenly disappear from view, thought it is actually still there, and not "dematerialized," as some individuals would have one believe. There is also another explanation of these sudden disappearances. As the field strength is varied, ionization may shift through every color of the spectrum. Increased energy causes the field to shift up past the visible portion of the spectrum, obscuring the craft from view, the same as a heavy cloud bank obscures a plane.

The intense resonating field also serves as a shield to deflect space debris from the ship. At the same time a blend is automatically set up between this field and atmosphere or space through which a spacecraft may be moving, thus preventing friction of any kind. Because of this pro-gravitic nature in its operation, occupants of a space ship are not affected by any violent maneuver or uncomfortable atmospheric conditions.

To travel at speeds faster than light, the ship's field is tuned to a high resonant point and the craft achieves "prime merge." For this, the ship is equipped with an automatic robot detector and control system, designed with provisions for manual control.

Contrary to accepted theories, matter is not converted to pure energy under such conditions. A ship within its force field can be compared to a planet within its atmosphere, moving as a unit through space. So, when a space ship accelerates and seems to disappear, it has merely achieved prime merge and its force field is vibrating at a speed faster than visible light. At higher frequencies it may become transparent to radar signals also.

The "hole" effect seen in many saucer photos is created by a "magnetic window." One small portion of the ship's force field is neutralized, permitting visual and radar-type observation. At times this is necessary when the force field of the craft is at a fairly high resonance.

The three-ball undercarriage seen on most saucers serves both as a retractable landing gear and as a "three-point electrostatic propulsion-control system." The mother ships use a series of bands built into the framework for the same control purpose. As we use retro-rockets to steer a rocket vehicle, the saucers use their variable three-point systems to maneuver by regulating the charge.

In horizontal flight within a planet's ionosphere, saucers travel along the planet's geomagnetic lines of force. They turn abruptly by shifting the ball-charge. In this way they are guided into and utilize the eddy currents found throughout space. A change of direction in the movement of a spacecraft may appear as a sudden 90-degree turn, or any of the erratic maneuvers so often ascribed to the saucers.

One important factor that our engineers for spacecraft will have to take into consideration is the multiple-wall construction required for safety purposes, as well as storage room for a large percentage of their propulsion equipment. There must be a minimum of two charged walls. The outer, negative wall comes in direct contact with the protective force field created around the ship. By its very nature this electrostatic force field ionizes all particles of matter near the ship's surface, and negatively charges space debris coming within its field of influence. The greater the amount of power used, the farther this influence extends from the ship.

A positive reference field is established in an inner wall, leaving the central portion of the ship at a neutral potential.

Important too is an automatic filtering and air-conditioning system installed between walls of a ship to purify the air and keep temperatures and pressures within the craft at a comfortable state for all persons aboard.

Actually, there is not too much difference between modern spacecraft and our own submarines that can surface on the water where outside pressures are light, or go to great depths where pressures against the ship are intense. At any depth a submarine can maneuver at will, without harm or discomfort to its occupants. So it is with a space ship. In outer space the pressures against it are light. When it enters a planet's ionosphere and approaches the planet, pressures intensify. Yet, wherever it is, it can maneuver at will without harm or discomfort to its occupants.

As our submarine navigators have had to become acquainted with the many rivers flowing beneath the surface of the ocean, so our space navigators will have to learn the magnetic lanes of outer space, as well as those between a planet

and its ionosphere. Temperatures, flow and currents throughout the Cosmos vary continually, in repeated patterns. These
space lanes will have to be used for direction of travel, and
the energy they generate will have to be converted into propulsion power if we ever hope to safely travel and enjoy interplanetary relationships with our neighbors on other planets.

4 RECENT DEVELOPMENTS

THE UNITED STATES and Russia are without doubt the leaders
in the conquest of space. Many "firsts" can be claimed by
both countries. America has approximately ten times more
satellites in orbit than Russia. We have the first successful
weather satellite; Russia had the first successful space probe.
Our probes are considered more sophisticated, as we have
miniature transistor circuitry that allows us to achieve good
results without the use of heavy payloads. Our sources of
information indicate that Russia is ahead on high-thrust rockets but behind in scientific instrumentation.

On March 6, 1960, the Los Angeles *Times* reported that information had been received from an ex-Soviet missile man,
to the effect that Russia had twice successfully tested a giant
nuclear rocket. The report originated from Hamburg, Germany. The informer has since vanished, after talking to two
United States intelligence men, and confirmation is not likely.
If the Russians have successfully tested a nuclear rocket, this
puts them from five to eight years ahead of our own pro-
jected program.

Russia launched her first lunar probe on January 2, 1959.
This probe, believed by our scientists to be aimed at the
moon, apparently missed and went on to successfully orbit
the sun. But was it an accident? Some evidence exists to
show that the probe was never intended to hit the moon. It
it possible that it was used to photograph the far side of the
moon at least eight months before the celebrated moon shot
that is given credit for taking the pictures.

While in Holland, prior to October 4, 1959, I heard an
announcement over the BBC from England which stated
that the Russians had discovered vegetation on the far side
of the moon. The Russian astronomer quoted also said that

35

the moon was not composed of volcanic ash as had been supposed but instead was made up of decomposed granite, the same as the earth. How could they have known of the vegetation on the moon's far side unless they had photographs from Lunik I? If they did take photos with Lunik I, it is reasonable to assume that they retouched them before release to the United States. They certainly wouldn't want us to know what they had discovered, as they want to be first to the moon and probably will try to claim it as Soviet territory. The pictures taken by Lunik III are probably still being kept secret.

Lloyd Mallan, nationally-known space photography specialist and science writer, has charged that the Russian photos are a fake. He has detected brush strokes on the pictures and states that some areas look like charcoal drawings. (From *Astronautics* magazine, June, 1960: "Russian moon photo found authentic by Rand Corporation, Santa Monica scientist Merton E. Davies.")

Russia may have retouched the photos before releasing them. I doubt if they faked them entirely as they must have known we will be taking pictures ourselves and would be able to show them up for what they were. The reason behind the retouching may be to keep secret the vegetation, trees and buildings of the space people based on the moon's far side. Just as our government doesn't tell all it knows, so the Russian government doesn't tell all it has found out.

A mapping engineer in Southern California found something very familiar about the Russian photos when they were released after October 6, 1959.

From the illustration on the Hungarian stamp, printed in January 1959, it is quite evident the Russians had photographed the far side of the moon prior to October 4, 1959. If the photo was indeed taken eight months earlier, then what was accomplished on the Lunik III trip of October 4, 1959?

It is entirely possible the Russians took better pictures that have not been released. Lunik III passed within 4,350 miles of the moon and we are told that no pictures were taken until the rocket was 42,000 miles away. Why were the pictures not taken while it was close to the moon? I believe they were as I have outlined previously.

The payload of Lunik III weighed a total of 614 pounds. In the third stage of the Russian rocket were 344 pounds of instruments and power supplies. The big question is: What happened to the 344 pounds of equipment in the third stage?

Jodrell Bank Radio Telescope in England tracked the Soviet signals for four days. The first two days, all transmission was normal at frequencies of 183.6 and 39.986 megacycles. On the third day, when the rocket was 4,350 miles from the moon's far side, all kinds of strange things began to happen.

According to *Electronics* magazine for October 23, 1959, "no transmission was received on 39.986 mc. Strong signals on 183.6 mc were received two minutes ahead of schedule and were characterized by a sequence not previously used by the Russians, consisting of 15-second signals spaced 15 seconds apart on the carrier wave. After 20 minutes the transmission changed to irregular sequences on two very closely spaced frequencies, lasting about 36 minutes.

"After that a steady signal resumed and lasted about 40 minutes until transmission ended. Two hiccups were heard later."

On the fourth day Jodrell Bank picked up the 183.6 mc transmission normally but received 39.986 mc for only two minutes, one hour after transmission on the first frequency began. The conclusion reached by our scientists was that Russia has probably landed an instrument package on the moon that even now may be sending back information. Some reports are already filtering back to me of strange signals coming back to Earth from the moon. The conjecture is they are from the Russian instrument package.

Is it possible that Russia landed a man on the moon some time ago? According to Soviet rocket specialist George Pokrovsky, in a statement released during February, 1960: "The possibility of disaster [in landing and taking off from planets] is not greater than in the case of aviation test pilots."

Professor Pokrovsky concluded: "There are no obstacles, in principle, to ensuring the exact functioning of mechanical equipment over great distances, even at the moon."

Since we have verified the existence of lunar atmosphere, is it possible that an earthman is now living on the moon?

Two U.S. scientists recently reported to the first International Space Science Symposium in Nice, France, that the moon has an atmosphere. Their theory is that the moon has a cold atmosphere composed of neutral hydrogen and minute quantities of argon. The thing to keep in mind is that the moon has a pronounced bulge on this side. This means that the altitude will be higher than on the other side. As a result it will have less vegetation and lighter air than will be found on the far side. By checking a globe of the world we find that most of the earth's great deserts are on one side of the planet. So the moon is following a similar pattern.

A very unusual thing occurred in Argentina early in February of 1960. For three weeks the Argentine Navy and the United States "experts" depth-bombed and called for the surrender of two mysterious submarines. These so-called submarines lay in the bottom of Golfo Nuevo, a narrow bay separated from the ocean by a narrow entrance. They were chased by the Argentines all over the bay and each time they were trapped they managed to slip mysteriously away. They were able to stay submerged for several days at a time and finally Argentine Navy Secretary Gaston Clemente told newsmen that "the patrol in the Nuevo Golfo will be called off."

These events occurred in a bay so compact that a good skindiver should have been able to polish off the sub with a few well-placed delayed-action charges. Yet all the mighty Argentine Navy, even with modern United States equipment and advice, was unable to do the job.

I had my ideas, but could not answer the questions asked until I received an explanation from the space travelers themselves. This came several weeks later, after the event was well silenced and events of the day were occupying people's attention.

The answer was that they were spacecraft. They were studying the bottom of the ocean to learn about conditions on our planet that are not yet indicated on dry land areas. A number of such craft are making a thorough study of underwater lands and naval ships of many nations have encountered them. For the most part, confidential, official reports of such encounters have been described as "fantastic." But here again, although our friends would like to surface

38

and make themselves, and what they are doing, known, our fears keep us in a state of hostility that prevents their doing so. Instead, they pass their findings on to others of their people who are working among our scientists and in other important places throughout the world. In turn, and in time, this information will be given to the people as findings from IGY research. Yet it is with their help that we are able to keep better informed on changes taking place within our planet as it continues on its natural course and undergoes its natural changes.

In the meantime American space probes were revealing much new information about outer space. America's Pioneer V uncovered a batch of major new space findings. These discoveries are shedding new light on the physical nature of the universe. They will help solve problems about the sun's influence on our weather and communications, and give additional data on the radiation bands found around our planet.

The first direct observation of pure cosmic rays was accomplished. The observations were made at a distance of three million miles from the earth. Pioneer V was riding through a storm of such rays kicked up by a huge sunspot. Evidence that the earth's magnetic field acts like a superpower dynamo to help feed radiation particles from the sun to the earth was also found. Pioneer V gave definite confirmation of the existence of a gigantic current of electricity encircling the earth at between 28,000 and 52,000 miles' altitude, seething with a current of five million amperes.

An entirely new and "disturbed" magnetic field in space at between 40,000 and 60,000 miles from the earth, and entirely independent of the earth's own field, was also discovered. This shows that the interplanetary boundary of the earth's own field is twice as far out as previously supposed.

A new Air Force discovery was announced by the Air Force Cambridge Research Center of Bedford, Massachusetts. A new photography technique has produced maps of the moon that show its surface is "no more rugged than that of Earth." Five thousand photographs were taken, using timing instruments to record the march of shadows from various prominences across the face of the moon. The program director, Charles F. Campen, stated that "steep slopes or towering rocks are absent from the lunar surface," although there may be some exceptions. Pictures of the moon for years have shown it to be a mass of cliffs, but the new technique, the Air Force said, indicates that this is not true.

Another first for the United States was the obtaining of X-ray photographs of the sun. This was accomplished by the United States Navy with a rocket fired 130 miles above New Mexico.

At the same time this was going on, Dr. Wernher von Braun, the space scientist, said that it is likely that life exists in the universe outside the earth. He said he foresaw an eventual meeting of an earth astronaut with "another being in space." In a speech to the Bureau of Advertising of the American Newspaper Publishers' Association, von Braun stated: "There is good reason to assume, on purely scientific grounds and on evidence by observation, that life of some kind exists elsewhere in the universe. In my opinion it is an entirely logical assumption. . . .

"But I suggest," he also said, "that it will be an even more memorable occasion when the first American meets another being in space. We can hope the greeting will be 'Hello, Earthman' and not 'Welcome, Tovarisch.'" He went on to say that one of the United States' three ultimate purposes was to "search for the origin of life and its likely presence outside the earth."

Our scientists are just now admitting that the natural force of gravity can be controlled, and that the ultimate control mechanism will be some form of electronic device. This was brought out by Donald C. Hoefler writing in *Electronic News* magazine for May 2, 1960. His source of information was Charles Tilgner, Jr., chief aeronautical engineer of Grumman Aircraft Engineering Corporation, Bethpage, N.Y. He also listed fourteen other companies engaged in some type of gravity research.

Now that minds have been turned in the right direction, it should not be long before some startling new ideas become apparent in the electronics industry. When the secret of gravity is finally revealed, the answer will be so simple that scientists will wonder why a schoolboy didn't think of it. Perhaps the answer has been published and the closed minds of today rejected or refused to consider it.

American satellites and rocket probes have accumulated so much data that it will take at least ten years to digest and catalogue the material. Of eleven American satellites still orbiting the earth, six are still transmitting back valuable information. The Soviet has three still in orbit, all silent.

Vanguard I has redrawn the face of the world and revealed that the earth is not round, as previously believed, but pear-shaped, as Columbus believed in 1492. Explorer VII sent back 300 miles of telemetered tape with information on trapped radiation and cosmic radiation showing a relationship between activity on the sun and geomagnetic storms on the earth.

Tiros, the weather satellite, has opened a new era in weather forecasting. It gives 400 photographs a day of the earth's cloud cover and enables man to have his first look at global weather.

Transit I-B is the world's first navigational satellite. Its main use is to serve as a fixed star for navigational purposes. The present Transit is the first of four and perhaps others will be in orbit by the time you read this.

Midas II has proved the feasibility of a "spy-in-the-sky" satellite that can soon take the place of the now defunct U-2 spy flights. With its infra-red sensor it can peer over 1,000 miles of territory a second as it orbits 300 miles above the earth. With results like these our science books are being thoroughly rewritten.

New findings about spiral galaxies in space have been reported by Caltech astronomer Dr. Guido Munch. Giving a more complete picture of the evolutionary processes of galaxies, the findings involve the movements of huge clouds of gas outward from the nucleus of the galaxy. These huge clouds were found to consist of oxygen and hydrogen. If these vast clouds of oxygen and hydrogen exist in the remote galaxies, it is likely that life-bearing planets have evolved there also, as they would have the environment necessary to acquire Earth-like atmospheres.

On March 13, 1960, the American public awoke to read a news item from New Mexico headlined: AIR FORCE

CHECKING CRASHED SPACE SHIP. The organization releasing the report, Aerial Phenomena Research Organization, had notified Air Force officials in Washington that the group had in its possession actual physical evidence that flying saucers were of extra-terrestrial origin. They offered to submit the material to the Air Force for scientific study.

Many people have wondered about the incident and what had happened. Few newspapers carried the follow-up on the story. The Air Force agreed to accept the evidence but only on their own terms. This would have enabled them to suppress their actual findings and announce to the world that APRO was indulging in a hoax. Rightfully APRO declined the Air Force offer.

The material that APRO had offered for analysis was acquired from some molten metal that fell over Campinas, Brazil in 1953. Some saucers were hovering over the town in full view of the citizens. One in the middle appeared to be in trouble. As in a similar incident a few years ago in Tacoma, Washington, the crippled saucer discharged some molten material. Pounds of it fell on streets and sidewalks and solidified into a shiny metal. The details of this incident were fully reported in South American newspapers but were kept from reaching the wire services in America.

The metal, according to the report I received, was analyzed by both a Brazilian laboratory and a scientist in the United States. It was pure tin (some reports said magnesium) which is known only in microscopic quantities on the earth. It was positive proof that the technology which produced it was not of this earth.

5. CHANGES IN OUR SYSTEM

RECENTLY I READ a bulletin from one of the many saucer "cults" that stated that vast changes were to take place upon the earth. When these changes occurred, the space people were supposed to fly down and rescue a chosen few out of the world. Nothing could be further from the truth.

True, there are changes occurring upon the earth. Our scientists are well aware of these, and many articles are appearing on the subject in an effort to alert the people of the world to just what is taking place. The IGY was organized in an attempt to learn more about the earth and its environment.

Some of these changes occurring at this time and those which will occur in the near future are natural results of happenings that periodically affect all planets. Earthquakes have always been with us and are a natural phenomenon. Lately they have been coming with greater frequency, and in areas usually not afflicted by this phase of Nature. They are a little more severe due to changes going on outside our planet as well as within.

Misery and death have always been present at such times. Contrary to the psychic messages supposedly being received from space people, these deaths are not the result of punishment by God but are due to being in the wrong place at the right time. When any certain person, chosen at random, dies in a quake or other "acts of God," it is due only to the accident of his or her happening to be there at that particular time. It could just as well have been you or anybody else.

If the public would heed warnings of scientists or would pay attention to feelings they might get urging them to leave a certain area, the number of these deaths would be greatly decreased.

In nature we find that the animals are warned ahead of time of certain coming disasters. We are warned in the same way through our impressions or feelings, but we usually ignore such things. Many lives were recently lost in Japan because a tidalwave warning was ignored by thousands of people. Others were saved from destruction because of strong feelings of disaster that they experienced before the event. New York subway officials have commented upon the fact that, on the days a wreck occurred, a lot of regular passengers were missing. Inquiry revealed they had had inner "warnings" not to ride those particular days. Where do these feelings originate, and why? They originate from the same source as the feelings which alert animals to danger. This is why rats will desert a ship that is going to sink, or animals will flee an area where a fire or flood is going to occur. The term for such alertness to coming events is "precognition."

Several reasons exist at this time to explain why we have had the sudden increase in natural phenomena such as earthquakes, hurricanes, tornados, etc.

On October 24, 1959, Dr. Harold D. Babcock, of Mt. Wilson and Palomar Observatories, announced that the polarity of the sun's magnetic field had reversed itself. The reversal was slow, taking nearly a year to complete. Before the reversal, the polarity of the sun's field was opposite to that of the earth's. This change in polarity will affect the earth in many ways. It will cause the interacting fields of space to attempt a similar change. The earth's field will be attempting to remain as it is, due to the continued motion of the earth in its orbital path. The conflict between the earth trying to remain the same and the reversed field trying to change it, will cause pressures to be exerted that were not apparent before. These will cause new earthquakes in many places that ordinarily are free from such events. Our weather patterns will make abrupt changes as the fields of the earth gradually change, due to air currents going in new directions. The rivers in the oceans will take new courses, and this will cause changes in ocean temperatures, with resulting changes in the types of marine life found in given areas.

The ocean changes are already apparent. Because of changes in temperature, fish formerly caught off California are being caught off Alaskan shores. Sharks are moving into areas of the seas where they were previouly unknown. The California climate has turned cooler and damper than in previous years.

Other things are starting to happen, independent of Nature. These are due to our rocket and satellite experiments. Although these experiments are necessary for the successful conclusion of our scientific program, all are affecting the earth to a slight degree. These slight changes are being noticed by many people in various countries.

Outer space may be compared to a vast sea in a state of apparent inertia. It has great activity within itself, activity so great as to be incomprehensible to our scientific instruments. Without understanding, it may be called stillness.

When a rocket ship or satellite passes through, it disturbs this so-called peaceful state, and this produces aftereffects upon Earth as well as all the other planets in our system. These effects are usually described as changing weather, or disturbed atmospheric conditions, and are manifest to most people only as a feeling of slight uneasiness. The atmosphere feels heavy and still to them and they can't figure out why they feel as they do. This is not dangerous, but as humans we become aware of that to which we are unaccustomed. These conditions will increase as more satellites and space ships come and go with our advancement into space.

Eventually, by the time we feel the space program has been established, Earth's people will have become accustomed to such changes and will consider conditions normal again.

A good example of this is a person who has lived for years in one room without a change of any kind. He has become a part of that room and with the feeling of being united with it. The air currents are the same day after day, just like the furnishings.

One day he decides to change the furniture around. Immediately the entire feeling of the room is changed. Air currents that normally follow certain paths are rerouted. Consciously, we are not alerted to these minute changes of air currents. Our subconscious minds are alerted, however, and as a result we sense a subtle difference in our surroundings. The minute radiation patterns of the objects in the room are also different, and we sense these as well.

Exactly the same thing is going on in space. Our space ships and satellites are disturbing the patterns of space, altering pressures, and causing the vastness of space to be agitated differently. We, as humans, sense these small changes and they make us feel uneasy.

The most dangerous disturbance of our atmosphere and space is not made by our ships or satellites. It is made by explosions which cause violent upheavals instead of harmonious agitation of our space-atmosphere environment. We all know that weather conditions change greatly while a war is going on. This is caused by pressure waves from the explosions reacting upon the normal pressures and densities of our atmosphere. We know that small quantities of matter from a rain-making plane can cause thousands of tons of water to fall in a very short time. In some of our nuclear explosions, whole islands were hurled aloft as minute particles. In one case, about three cubic miles of matter was lofted skyward. This great quantity of matter is going to filter down very slowly for decades; and when it does, it affects the weather in general.

The changes in the earth's force field brought about by the hydrogen explosions, combined with the changes caused by the sun's reversal of polarity, will cause disturbances for many years. There will even be earth disturbances such as earthquakes, tidal waves, etc., due to these terrific distortions of the natural conditions of space. Even the explosions resulting from separating various stages of our rockets will cause some disturbance.

Some day, when we learn to harness natural forces for these purposes, such conditions of change will be eliminated, but we cannot expect normal weather while the pioneer experiments of today are going on. People should not fear these changes, but rather should learn to understand them. That is the price of progress. Once we have established space travel, things will appear to return to normal. They will be different from before, but will be recognized as normal because everyone will be accustomed to the change. The world and the Solar System alter their position in relation to man's progress. This may seem dangerous, but is not when properly understood. All progress appears dangerous at first.

As an example, when man undertakes to build a highway through the wilderness, he never knows what might be encountered. He feels isolated and anything can be expected to happen. As he goes along he finds areas where he has to blast and other areas where he moves with ease. He learns as he progresses, even with sacrifices. Once the trees, shrubs, rocks, etc., are removed and the highway completed, the entire atmosphere of the wilderness changes. People drive along the highway with no feeling of insecurity or apprehension. Families stop and have picnics where before danger seemed to lurk. The once forbidding forest is now a park where children laugh and play.

This is what is taking place in space and in our atmosphere at this time. As we venture outward we find some areas that must be "blasted," others wherein we move with ease.

Areas that seem dangerous now will one day be tourists' delights. As it is on Earth, so it is in space.

In the end the society of the world and system will blend with its environment and with greater understanding move forward. We must keep our goal in mind regardless of appearances for the attainment is worth all the sacrifices.

6. THE SYMBOLS

ALL PLANETS within our system are inhabited. As within a human family, so it is within a system of planets—individual development varies, also its effects. It is not surprising that humans on our sister planets have learned lessons which differ from those we have learned on Earth. People who have achieved progress without wars have naturally advanced beyond those who repeat their destructive practices through civilization after civilization.

Through the years, archeologists in our world have unearthed many relics of past civilizations, some indicating progress beyond that which we know today—in the field of alchemy, for instance. In many instances, and from remote parts of the world, strange characters have been found inscribed on rocks. Books have been written on these findings, and men are constantly seeking a better understanding of those who left such records. Still, the context of some of these symbols often can only be guessed, since they are remnants of unknown and as yet untraceable languages.

As the search continues, with more and more buried cities being unearthed in widely separated parts of the world, a pattern seems to be forming to connect many of the finds.

On November 20th, 1952, when I had the great pleasure of meeting a man from Venus on a California desert, near Desert Center, he had symbols on the soles of his sandals. These were left in the earth where we stood, and, as told in my report in *Flying Saucers Have Landed,* plaster casts were made of his footprints.

Some friends and I had gone to the desert on this day in the hope of securing photographs of spacecraft. I had received many reports of their coming close to the ground in such areas. Although I did not question that these craft were manned by human beings like ourselves, it was beyond my fondest hope to meet one of them.

When the Scout craft came in close, I quickly took pictures of it and hoped they would be good, since I was not then—nor am I today—a professional photographer. These were plates, and I put each one in my jacket pocket as I took it from my camera. It takes no stretch of the imagination to realize my excitement, as well as the strain under which I labored to talk with this man, since apparently, he did not understand our language. Communication had to be by means of telepathy.

After carrying on a conversation in this manner for several minutes, we approached his waiting ship, which was not far away. In spite of his warning to stay away from the hovering craft, I turned to speak to him and got my shoulder caught in the power emanating from the Scout, whose outer edge was a little above my head. Although I realized I might suffer harm from this radiation, my greatest concern was for the exposed film plates in my jacket pocket. Automatically I took these out of my pocket to put them in one on my other side.

As I did so, this friendly man from Venus extended his hand as a request for one. I understood his gesture and held them all out for him to help himself. He took one.

Upon returning home and sending the film to my photographer for processing, I found that all of the negatives were blurred, much as if they had been exposed to X-ray.

Twenty-three days after this first meeting, the Scout returned—this time to my home—and I was able to take some good pictures, using my telescope with my camera. Imagine my surprise when the little ship approached close to where I was standing! A porthole opened and my friend dropped the encased negative which he had taken after our first meeting. Upon processing by my photographer, the original exposure was found to have been washed off and symbols, similar in character to those in his footprints, were in its place.

At the time I had no idea concerning the message these symbols contained. Nor did I know of others anywhere on Earth. As the years have passed, many people throughout the world have endeavored to decipher them. Most of these, however, were psychic in nature and far from being accurate, according to information from the space travelers.

In 1956, while vacationing in Mexico, I received a letter from Spain, telling of a man there who had a personal meeting with a man from a Scout ship, and inquiring if it could have been the same space visitor who had met me in the desert in 1952. In this case, the visitor had given the Spaniard a beautiful and strange stone on which unfamiliar characters had been carved. A photograph of the stone enclosed in the letter showed the symbols to be similar to those I had been given.

Within the past couple of years I have learned of a book, *Die Sohne der Sonne,* by Marcel F. Homet, in which is reproduced a plate of symbols found in Argentina. In certain respects this plate of symbols is identical to those on the negative dropped from the Scout. This book is published in German only, so far as I can find out, and deals with ancient culture in the Amazon area. Thus another link is added to the chain of facts tying interplanetary communications and relations with past civilizations on Earth, whose records for the most part have become lost through the centuries or were destroyed deliberately.

One of the main reasons for these symbols being given to me was to provide the "concrete" evidence that the space travelers knew our people demand. Since many of them have developed their natural talent of telepathy far beyond our understanding on Earth, they actually know us better than we know ourselves. This is because when any of them decide to come to Earth, either for short visits or long stays, they take the time and effort to become well acquainted with our customs and ways of thinking.

They knew that the photographs which I had taken of their ships would serve well for some. On the other hand, there would be many—as there were—who would declare that they were the results of my imagination, that I had built models and photographed them. Of course this has been proven false, and today several nations are building craft of the same design as the Scouts, which were first said to be contrary to all laws of aerodynamics, and thus incapable of space travel.

The symbols would add weight to the evidence of the photographs, and also serve as a necessary link between our present experiences with interplanetary visitors and ancient records now being unearthed.

As might be expected, there have been a few sincere people who have worked long and hard for a factual interpretation of this writing from another world.

One, a scientist in Africa, worked with prints of the symbols, both those on the negative and those in the footprints, before coming up with an interpretation that was confirmed by the Brothers. By using each symbol on the negative as a piece for a jigsaw puzzle, he was able to construct a diagram for a Scout. Adding the symbols in the footprints, he secured the pattern for a large mother ship. As he continued studying and rearranging the symbols, he received ideas regarding the propulsion used in these craft, and the manner in which the power was controlled. As he put his ideas into experimental research, he reported amazing progress, although he did not give me any details.

When I last heard from this man about a year ago, he was still working with the symbols and stated that his experiments had led him into certain "unscientific" findings that he was keeping in notes. When he had the time and opportunity, he planned on writing a text book on his findings, since, he said, they would drastically change a number of presently accepted theories. After accomplishing this, he hoped to visit me in America. I am looking forward with interest to his visit.

From Japan I received a beautiful scroll in which, so far as I could get it translated, the symbols were interpreted in relation to some of the ancient history and philosophies of certain parts of the Orient.

The Brothers have acknowledged that some history of ancient civilizations on Earth as well as some of the philosophy of those civilizations, which conforms to that known on their planets and lived today by the people there, were included in the symbols.

So, although even today I am unable to give a complete explanation of the symbols left with me so many years ago, perhaps they have served their purpose. The Brothers express satisfaction. Yet, as we progress spaceward and eventually reach our neighboring planets, we in time will learn their languages—and then the full import of the symbols from space, as well as those ancient ones from our own planet, will be learned by the people of Earth.

7. ANSWERS FOR THE SKEPTICS

WHEN THE SATELLITES and high-altitude balloons began to relay accurate data from outer space, quite a few revisions had to be made in scientific thinking. This chapter deals with a few of those revisions.

Those readers who have followed the see-saw course of acceptance and rejection pursued by officials when the spacecraft appeared, will recall how certain die-hard skeptics tried to shout down or explain away the sightings and contacts.

When *Flying Saucers Have Landed* was published in 1953, describing my first contact with a visitor from the planet Venus, the skeptics brought out huge files of data to "prove conclusively" that life could not exist on that planet, because its atmosphere supposedly contained no water and no oxygen, only cardon dioxide.

The discovery of water vapor in the atmosphere of Venus by U. S. scientists, during November 1959, led the experts to concede that some sort of life "might" exist on Venus. Within two weeks, scientists who participated in a news conference at NASA headquarters in Washington, D.C., agreed that life on Venus seemed "more probable" as a result of the discovery that the planet's atmosphere contains water vapor.

From *Astronautics* magazine, April 1960, page 8:

"John Strong of Johns Hopkins has found more water vapor above the cloud layer of Venus than in the Earth's own stratophere. 15 to 30 microns on Venus to 6 on Earth."

During February 1960, a surprising statement was issued. Dr. Edward G. Pendray, founder of the American Rocket Society, stated: "Venus may turn out to be a wonderful place to live. We don't know much about its surface, because we can't see it. But it is about the same size as Earth and nearer to the Sun. It may be like Florida all over."

Spokesmen for the die-hard factions then clamored that

life as Earthmen know it could not exist on Venus, because its atmosphere supposedly contains too much carbon dioxide and the planet's surface temperature is too high. Shortly after this statement was released to the public, scientists announced their discovery of heat zones above the earth's atmosphere, with temperatures ranging above 1,000 degrees Fahrenheit. They admitted the heat belts could prevent any accurate measurement of another planet's surface temperature.

An interesting fact on planetary atmosphere was brought to light during January, 1960, by Dr. Roger Revelle of the Scripps Institute of Oceanography in La Jolla, California. Dr. Revelle stated that Earthmen are greatly increasing the amount of carbon dioxide in their atmosphere as they burn more coal, oil and natural gas. He predicted an increase of perhaps 20 per cent in atmospheric carbon dioxide in the next 100 years; that could mean a 100 per cent increase in Earth's atmospheric carbon dioxide in less than 500 years! Perhaps our scientists will discover there is a relationship between the amount of carbon dioxide in a planet's atmosphere and the age of that planet's civilization.

When I first stated that people on Venus enjoy far better health and a longer life span than Earth's inhabitants, my statements were instantly ridiculed.

Another new theory was presented in January, 1960, by Dr. Vincent Askey, then President-elect of the American Medical Association. Dr. Askey reported to his colleagues that Earthmen now stand at the threshold of an age in which they will be able to control evolution. He said that within fifty years, Earth people could develop into a race of supermen with perfect health, high intelligence and a life expectancy of 125 years.

You could hear the skeptics snickering around the world when I stated in *Inside the Space Ships** that the moon has an atmosphere.

Information radioed back from the Russian rocket which landed on the moon in 1959 apparently sobered a few scoffers.

According to *Aviation Week* magazine, the rocket reported

*published as *Inside the Flying Saucers* by Paperback Library, Inc. (# 53-428, 60¢)

that the moon is enveloped by a blanket or belt of low-energy ionized gases. The article suggested that a blanket of such gases would resemble an atmosphere.

What did American scientists think of this announcement? NASA's John Townsend said the discovery of an ionosphere above the moon was very significant and surprising to him. "The detection of an ionosphere at a relatively high distance from the moon means that the moon has a definite atmosphere, a condition that a few scientists could only guess at before," Townsend stated.

When I said that the space people had told me our solar system has twelve planets, instead of nine as we previously believed, the skeptics openly scoffed.

In February, 1960, Russian astronomers at the Kazakhstan Astrophysical Institute announced they had confirmed the existence of another planet beyond the orbit of Pluto, which had been previously termed the "outermost planet" of our solar system. Questioned on their reaction to the Russian claim, American astronomers asked for more details so they could check for themselves. Dr. Gustav Bakos of the Smithsonian Institute in Boston said the irregularities in Pluto's orbit have suggested there might be another planet beyond; similar irregularities in the orbit of Neptune led to the discovery of Pluto in 1930.

When I related meeting a man from the planet Mars, in *Inside the Space Ships,* that statement was ridiculed.

During 1959, a science editor for United Press International reported: "The most refined test to date of whether there is life on the planet Mars has added to the evidence that there is. But the evidence is still far from conclusive . . . ."

Dr. William Sinton of Lowell Observatory has already concluded, with the help of the 200-inch Hale Telescope on Mount Palomar, that the dark regions on Mars may be great patches of vegetation, some of it similar to that on Earth.

Wells Webb, research scientist at the University of California, stated in 1958 that, because of their complex geometric designs, the famed Martian canals were definitely constructed by intelligent beings.

Then in 1960, we read a statement published by Russian physicist I. S. Shklovsky, who said he believed the two moons of Mars, Phobos and Deimos, are artificial satellites. Shklovsky based his opinions on studies of their highly reflective surfaces and accentric orbits, which indicate Phobos and Deimos are hollow, man-made satellites.

The old arguments that life "as Earthmen know it" could not exist on other planets of our solar system were based primarily on readings taken with two astronomical standbys: the spectrograph and the thermocouple.

This brings up another point for discussion.

Strange reports have been radioed from American and Russian satellites orbiting the earth. They "conclusively proved" that life as we know it could not exist on Earth! After analyzing our globe from outer space with astronomical spectrographs, the satellites reported: No oxygen or water vapor exists in Earth's atmosphere! The answer, according to our scientists, was that the electrified layer of our ionosphere effectively blocked the spectrum lines of oxygen and water. The lines simply did not register!

In view of their findings, and since a similar ionospheric shell exists around every planet, it is evident that spectrographic analysis of another planet's atmosphere cannot be termed reliable when it is taken from outside the planet's ionosphere. The spectrograph may be useful in analyzing light *emitted* from the sun and other stars, but it is obviously unreliable when used to study light *reflected* from another planet. Only space probes beneath the ionospheres of other planets will give us true measurements of their atmospheric conditions.

In regard to the thermocouple, its readings may be accurate when taken from outside our ionosphere; but, like the spectrograph, it is useless when operated within our ionospheric shell. After all, we have thermal bands around the earth that measure from 1,000 to 4,000 degrees Fahrenheit. I believe these bands would make our planet seem inhospitably warm to an extra-terrestrial observer.

Before we leave the topic of spectrums, let me put an end once and for all to wild rumors of "little green men" landing on earth from our solar planets.

The space people have told me the warm-blooded oxygen-breathing mammal we call Man exists throughout the Universe, with the same variety in facial features, coloring, height and weight as found on earth. Man is the most highly developed creature on every inhabited planet.

Nature has provided a protective filtration device for thin-skinned man which we call skin pigmentation. The pigments, which cause skin coloration, serve merely to filter out harmful portions of the solar radiation spectrum, thereby protecting sensitive tissues beneath the skin.

Our sun emits radiation that, in the atmospheres of solar planets, has a definite reddish cast. The filtering pigments screen out the "red" portion of the sun's spectrum and therefore our skin coloration tends toward "warm" colors: red, yellow, pink, bronze, and brown. It is remarkable that Earthmen have attached such false importance to skin coloration, when it merely serves as a natural protective device.

When I reported that the moon was being used as a base by space people, the skeptics replied that if there were people on the moon, we could see them from Earth; they also claimed humans could not survive on the "airless, waterless" lunar landscape.

At a space conference in Nice, France during January 1960, Dr. Harold C. Urey of the University of California told his colleagues "the moon may not be as dead as has been supposed." He said there is still reason to believe there is radiation around the moon (now a proven fact) which would suggest various life-giving components, including water, underneath the moon's surface.

Dr. Raymond Doetach of the University of Maryland stated in December, 1959 that the existence of some kind of life on the moon "could not be ruled out."

Soviet science writer F. Siegel echoed: "The concept of the moon as a dead world needs revision." Siegel referred specifically to "strange spots of changing color and location" which have been observed at the bottom of certain lunar craters.

On page 226 of *Inside the Space Ships** we read: "In the numerous large craters [of the moon] which you see from

---

*published as *Inside the Flying Saucers* by Paperback Library, Inc. (# 53-428, 60¢)

Earth, you will notice very large hangers. We have built these hangars on such a scale in order that much larger ships than this one can enter easily . . . when a ship enters these hangars, a process of de-pressurizing the passengers takes place. This requires about 24 hours . . ."

In the January, 1958 issue of *Sky and Telescope*, published by Harvard College Observatory, we find the following information on page 138: "In recent years, amateur astronomers have been paying increasing attention to lunar domes, small rounded 'hills' that are being observed in increasing numbers . . ."

The domes referred to above are white and look symmetrical as if they were turned out of chalk on a lathe. They have appeared in lunar craters over the past few years until now over 200 have been charted. And some astronomers still contend that nothing ever changes on the moon!

Astronomers previously claimed the moon was airless, yet even before the Russian rocket found lunar atmosphere, many observers had seen meteors flaring into incandescence as they approached the moon. An atmosphere must be present before friction such as that could exist. Walter Haas, astronomer at Ohio State University, reports he has observed meteor flashes above the moon, but no sign of impact, indicating that the moon has an atmosphere sufficient to burn up meteors.

Astronomers have estimated that up to 100,000 meteors per hour approach the moon. If the moon really had no atmosphere, these meteors should strike so hard as to radically alter the lunar landscape every hour. If this were to occur, the new craters could be readily observed through our telescopes, since the Russian rocket—which was only 87 inches long and 47 inches in diameter—made quite a splash itself.

The cloud of dust and gas that rose when the rocket landed was estimated to be from 310 to 560 miles high. Without an atmosphere, such clouds could not be raised.

When the first satellites radioed back their information, Earth's people were probably surprised to hear scientific reports which stated, in parallel terms, exactly what I had written in my books at least three years before.

For example, on page 76 of *Inside the Space Ships* I reported: "I was amazed to see that the background of space is totally dark. Yet there were manifestations taking place all around us, as though billions upon billions of fireflies were flickering everywhere, moving in all directions, as fireflies do. However, these were of many colors, a gigantic celestial fireworks display that was beautiful to the point of being awesome."

On page 77, I continued: "Space and its activity held me transfixed as I strained my eyes in an attempt to see everything that was going on . . . apart from the firefly effects, I saw a good many large luminous objects passing through space. The larger bodies, so far as I could tell, were not burning, but merely glowing."

The same findings were revealed by scientists in January, 1960: "Outer space is a dazzling vision of multi-colored brightness, not a black void, a Moscow radio science commentator reports. He says this was learned from the Soviet Sputniks and adds: 'It is very bright and colored like a rainbow because interplanetary gas shines with a multi-colored light, while thousands of millions of stars shine through it, forming almost solid looking pinky gold or dazzling white shapes.' "

A subsequent report from our own scientists stated that "space, instead of being an empty vacuum as formerly thought, is actually filled with billions of particles of matter, all in a constant state of activity and glowing with a weird fluorescence of their own."

In *Inside the Space Ships** I also told of huge radiation belts building up around the earth. The hazards they present were fully outlined on pages 91-92.

Three years later, in August 1958, we read in the newspapers: "Explorer IV is sending back quite startling revelations about an intense band of radiation far out in space, a project official said today. George Ludwig, an associate in the physics department of the State University of Iowa, said early data from Explorer IV shows that the radiation is lethal. Ludwig said above 1,200 miles the Roentgen ratings have been amazing."

*published as *Inside the Flying Saucers* by Paperback Library, Inc. (# 53-428, 60¢)

Once again we find valid evidence of prior knowledge, confirmed years later by scientific reports. Of course, I didn't call the radiation zones "Van Allen Belts"; I have never met the gentleman for whom they are named.

In *Flying Saucers Have Landed,* I reported that the space ships were magnetically propelled. Our scientists had previously demonstrated magnetic propulsion on a laboratory scale, but the skeptics were still unwilling to admit that flying saucers could be propelled by anything so simple (relatively speaking) as electromagnetism.

In November, 1959, the International Telephone and Telegraph Corporation announced that its scientists had developed a device which produced high voltage electricity from the radiant energy of a sunbeam. The firm said its device could produce extremely high voltages to provide power for propelling space ships.

A prominent physicist, Dr. Y. C. Lee, announced several months earlier that electrical propulsion could speed Earthmen through space at velocities "eventually reaching three million miles per hour."

On pages 237 and 238 of *Inside the Space Ships* we find an account of the tilting of the Earth's axis, wherein the space people stated our planet has already begun a slow, nearly imperceptible tilt.

According to the space travelers, the tilt is part of a cycle which occurs at regular intervals in every planet's development.

In February, 1960, scientists reported finding evidence at the South Pole of fern-like plants, spores, pollen, plant tissue, forest and even beds of coal (which is fossilized vegetation).

Dr. George Llano, American lichenologist, said this evidence indicates the South Pole received more sunlight in past centuries than it does now.

Dr. Lucy Cramwell of New Zealand said the evidence indicated that forests once grew in Antartica like those now common in southern South America. On the basis of this evidence, scientists believe a change may have occurred in the earth's axis of rotation.

While my statements have been critically received in some quarters, I have aided the scientists whenever possible. In return, many scientists have assisted me in the gentlemanly, dignified manner which befits any serious student of science.

Recent findings do not wholly prove my previous statements, but in their parallel pattern they conclusively prove the wisdom of keeping one's mind receptive to new knowledge.

8. RUMORS AND RUMOR MONGERS

I HAVE RECEIVED many letters from people who are confused by certain wild rumors that are, year after year, circulated against me. It is a mystery how some of these tales get started. A few are deliberate falsehoods apparently designed to discredit my experiences in the eyes of the public. Others are so absurd as to make one wonder about the mental status of the individuals who originate or spread such tales. Even people who do not accept the reality of my experiences refuse to believe some of these stories.

In December, 1958, a spaceman took me from a train near Kansas City, Missouri, and after driving me to his ship, we flew to Davenport, Iowa where I disembarked after dark. A nationally-known saucer publication charged that my story was a fabrication and proceeded to publish a distorted, nonfactual account of what was supposed to really have happened. Needless to say, most of this supposed exposé was outright fabrication itself.

The investigator for the publication was a man who claimed to be a contactee himself. He claimed communication by means of trance. People he talked to reported he used a phoney badge and impersonated an officer, which in itself is an illegal act. On one occasion he gathered a group of people, including some newsmen, at a place where a saucer was supposed to land. Up to the last he claimed to be in mental contact with the crew of the saucer. When it failed to appear, he was laughed out of the group he claimed to represent and turned to discrediting other groups and individuals.

It is entirely likely that the publication which used the investigator's phoney exposé of me was unaware of the man's record of falsehoods. The fact remains that no effort was made to correct the situation after the director of the organization was notified of the deception used against him. He has consistently pursued the same course in the past. Never once has he asked me about my claims; instead he jumps on any discrediting information and publishes it without verification.

This well-known, self styled UFO investigator, with headquarters in Washington, D.C., stated in his second book that I "ran a hamburger stand on the road to the Mount Palomar Observatory." He said I had a telescope "on the roof of the stand" and implied that running such a stand was detrimental to my scientific interests.

A mutual friend in Washington advised this fellow to pay me a visit, or at least spend a three-cent stamp, in order to get the true facts before publishing his book. Evidently he didn't feel it was worth the trouble.

Palomar Gardens Café has accommodated many notable visitors. These people, from all over the world, probably wouldn't have signed the guest register in a mere "hamburger stand." Many guests told Mrs. Alice K. Wells, the owner, that her café had been well recommended by friends, and was one of the highlights of their trip.

I have never owned a business, nor was I employed in any capacity at the Palomar Gardens Café. My wife and I lived on the property and I had set up my two telescopes there. One was a 15-inch reflector which stood in a nearby clearing. It was housed in a small dome observatory. The other, a six-inch reflector, was portable and could be carried in an automobile. This six-inch scope was the instrument used in photographing the pictures shown in my previous books. These were my own instruments and were in no way connected with the Palomar Observatory. Although I was acquainted with several scientists at the Palomar Observatory, I have never been employed as a member of the observatory, or even claimed to be a member of the observatory staff.

The observatory had no one to give out information, so many people would ask questions at the café in regard to its operation. I often conversed with guests in the café dining room, on astronomy and other topics. When the spacecraft arrived, I was in a position to answer many questions and to give free lectures for service clubs.

Some newspapers used the term "hamburger vendor" in a

derogatory sense, hinting I was a nobody who had "jumped on the Flying Saucer Bandwagon." Even if the reference to me had been true, it would not have been to my discredit, for America is built upon the little fellows who made good.

Palomar Gardens was far from a "hamburger stand," for it had been twice publicized in *Holiday* magazine.

I am going to relate a few more of the stories that have been circulated against me. It will not be easy to see how intelligent people could originate such absurd stories, much less get people to believe them. Many people seem to be looking for such things as these and spread them around knowing that many will believe it as gospel truth. If they hear of something that may give me a small boost in public opinion, they either discard it or distort it to suit their own purposes.

The editor of a national saucer magazine claimed a few months ago that I submitted a manuscript to him in 1944. In the manuscript, I supposedly depicted Jesus Christ coming to earth in a space ship. He insinuated that I rewrote the story in 1952 and renamed the pilot Orthon.

Nothing could be farther from the truth. In 1944 I knew nothing about spacecraft or space people. I was too busy helping to clear land on the slopes of Mount Palomar, to do any writing of any kind. I respect the name of Jesus Christ too highly to use it in that manner. Any one using the name of Christ in that manner is a blasphemer and has little or no respect for the name. For the hundreds who are using His name for financial gain, I have no respect whatsoever.

Another time it was reported that I had died and my daughter was running the business. This in spite of the fact that in thirty-seven years of married life, my wife and I had no children at all.

At 12:15 A.M., on the morning of August 8, 1959, it was reported by a visitor on an all-night radio program that, in my earlier years, I was a spiritualist who claimed to materialize Venusians who performed appendectomies upon patients. One of my co-workers wrote a letter to the M.C. of the program requesting an on-the-air interview to correct the wild falsehoods, but was not granted even the courtesy of a reply.

For the past seven years, certain groups have tried to discredit my photographs. At the same time they have published them in their psychic magazines and scientific laboratories have used them as a guide in constructing prototype space-craft. I can at least thank them all for acknowledging that I existed.

Many are making a good living from their writings. What would they write about if I had not shared my experiences?

Be it a brochure or the large papers, I can be thankful to them for keeping what I represent before the public, for they create a curiosity that makes people want to know what space is all about.

The opposition sponsored much adverse publicity, but the program of knowledge would not have been broadcast throughout the world today if it had not been for the opposition's unknowing assistance.

9. WHAT I HAVE LEARNED FROM INTERPLANETARIANS

THROUGH THE YEARS since I first met Orthon on a California desert, I have had many meetings with our space traveling friends. Some have been very casual and unexpected. Others I expected, much as I described in *Inside the Space Ships*.* Never have I been able to make definite appointments with them for a specific time and place, nor have I outgrown the inner exaltation of being in their company. However, even though I have had so many meetings with them, it would be as foolish for me to say that I know all who are on Earth, as is would be to say that I know everybody in any city or town. I have been told, that on many occasions I have been visited by and talked with space travelers without recognizing them, and without their identifying themselves. On a few occasions, I have later met one or two on a ship whom I recognized as having talked with previously, without recognition.

It is for this reason that I have so often said and written that many people, in fact untold numbers of people, have met and talked with space travelers without recognizing them. Many work in industries and government positions throughout the

*published as *Inside the Flying Saucers* by Paperback Library, Inc. (# 53-428, 60¢)

world. They may also be found in the armed forces of every nation, working in divisions of science, communications, medical corps, etc. where they are not required to be trained for slaughter of their fellowmen.

I have been asked endless times how this can be, when so many personal identifications are required of everyone nowadays. These are not insurmountable problems even to Earth's people. There are innumerable ways in which identifications can be established. If one questions this statement, let him start an investigation into the matter, and he may uncover many surprises for himself!

Often the space people are recognized as being above the average in their natural friendliness, and slowness to anger, and at times in their telepathic abilities. But since telepathy is a science in which many people on Earth have developed an interest, with more or less success in using, the space people in business are usually shrugged off as just good telepathists, or as having extremely strong hunches.

Let me here give a warning to the reader not to think everybody who uses telepathy, or follows his hunches or feeling impressions, is a space visitor. Keep balanced in all ways and accept a man for what he is, not as a possible god, as so many have catalogued the space people.

Since the publication of *Inside the Space Ships,* people throughout the world have turned to virtual worship of our visitors from other planets. I have received innumerable letters from those who want to meet them and be taken to another planet where they might evade the lessons of earth. This was not at all the purpose of the book.

As I have said, many of our meetings have been very casual —we would discuss Earth and her people, along with some of the problems we have created for ourselves, the same as you and I might do over a cup of coffee or a glass of beer.

In *Inside the Space Ships* it was said that, even under the best of conditions, Man sometimes develops a tendency toward arrogance, in spite of having been taught its penalties. This continues to take place occasionally throughout the Cosmos, on even the most highly developed planet of which we can conceive. Since Universal Law forbids Man to destroy Man, such people are still moved to more lowly planets where they may experience the penalty they have been taught awaits the arrogant, for it is a characteristic of mankind to remember better lessons learned through experience than by other methods of instruction. Earth long ago was chosen as the planet in our system to which such people were moved. But let me make clear one important point.

Because of this statement, many readers jumped to the conclusion that Earth is nothing more than a penal colony, and her inhabitants have little chance for joy and happiness. This is erroneous!

It is the working out of the Law and not personal decisions of other people. This point has been made very clear to me by the space people, whose understanding and compassion far surpass our limited conception. Our Earth was formed by the same Creator who built all the planets, suns and satellites that form endless numbers of systems throughout the Cosmos. It is as holy as any place in the entire universe. Earth is even more beautiful than many planets whose inhabitants have overcome destructive attitudes and have advanced socially and scientifically beyond us. If Man would take the time and effort to observe the beauty of Nature, wherever he might be, he could not help but recognize the many blessings bestowed upon Earthlings by the great Creator.

Even in the largest cities there are museums and parks with flowers, birds, trees, and even little insects of all kinds. These are all very beautiful if one will only take a few minutes to observe any one of them closely. Yet we have become so engrossed with the effort of living, and quite often with the passion for obtaining possessions, that greed has overtaken us and we turn our interests toward destruction of many kinds of little creatures.

On the other hand, people on Venus who have studied Nature closely have learned that all natural forms are created for a definite purpose. Therefore they do not use poison sprays, artificial fertilizers, etc. They have learned, as we are learning, that while certain insects are destroyed through poisons, others just as destructive, in the absence of their natural enemies, multiply prolifically. Subsequently, birds too become victims of their natural food being poisoned.

In order to help maintain a balance of fertility, small life forms were created. Because these eat a certain percentage of crops and plants, we now poison them, and today mankind is paying a heavy price in health.

Thus our lack of understanding of natural principles and causes, along with the greed to get all we can for our money and effort, has led us into a war with Nature. We have set up a chain reaction which, when traced, will be found to affect all life from the lowly insect to man himself.

Instead of the artificial fertilizers which have become so popular in our world, the farmers on Venus return to their earth a certain percentage of Nature's produce for mulching and fertilizing. To avoid bleeding the land of its fertility, they practice rotation of crops, and give their land periodic rests.

As a result of this care, the food they grow contains all the natural elements so vital for good health.

Points of this type have been brought out to me repeatedly, not in reprimand but as an analysis for many of the health conditions now existing on Earth that were not prevalent before poison wars were started against Nature's little creatures. When we return to a study of Nature, we too will learn that all things were created for a specific purpose. Because we have turned our interests away from the underlying cause of so many things, and have become absorbed in materialism, we have brought upon ourselves many conditions from which we must suffer until we return to Nature, understand her ways and purposes, and adjust our ways to conform with her principles.

Our planet is but one classroom. Here are lessons to be learned that can be found in no other planet in our system. There are, however, many duplicates of our system throughout the billions of galaxies comprising the Cosmos, as there are duplicates of systems lower in development than ours, and others higher. But as a child cannot solve the problems of a college man until he has learned the lessons of grammar and high schools, thus preparing himself for the college work, so Man cannot skip rungs on the ladder of life, avoiding certain lessons along the highway of progression.

We might compare Earth with a kindergarten where children of many personalities are gathered in work and play.

Here will be found the arrogant, aggressive type; the timid; the introvert and extrovert; the patient and the impatient; the kind and the cruel. It is the purpose of the kindergarten classes to teach these individuals to blend harmoniously with one another. In such a manner self-control is established and group coordination can be brought about.

Here too are taught primary principles in the purpose and operation of the body as a channel of expression of universal life and intelligence. The origin and power of thoughts, with the effects they can have on an individual and his surroundings is also learned. With increased understanding comes greater appreciation, joys and accomplishments.

Instead of recognizing the lessons our planet has for its people, we have been taught through the centuries that the human race is peculiar to Earth alone. As a result, rules have been set up by which we live without considering, or trying to learn of vaster rules existing thoughout the Cosmos.

The space travelers are as interested in us, our ways of thinking and acting, as any humanitarian would be. They come so that they might help us learn the universal laws of life, as a teacher works with her pupils. A successful teacher never talks down to his students. Through understanding their minds and manner of thinking, he endeavors to help the younger ones unfold intellectually. The space visitors serve in this same manner. They do not impose themselves upon us, nor do they take a superior attitude toward us. Rather, realizing that we do not understand the laws involved in our thoughts and acts, they live amongst us, hoping that, by their example of harmonious living, they can instil in us a desire to do the same.

I shall never forget the numbers of people who have visited me, loudly expressing their desire to get "out of this hell on Earth, to live in the peace and happiness of Venus." Yet when I asked these same people if they were willing to live as the Venusians, they were not. They did not want to give up their pet likes and dislikes. They like to feel that, for one reason or another, they are better than a fellow-being who may not have had the same education, may be of a different color of skin or religion, or may not have been so successful in a business and financial way. Still, it is likes and dislikes of this kind that keep Mankind on Earth divided against itself. There are no such divisions on Venus, although these same differences of color and intellectual unfoldment, even of occupation exist there as here. So if such people were taken there, with their present attitudes, they would find an even greater "hell" there than here, because they would be alone with their likes and dislikes until they willingly freed themselves from them.

There are those people on Earth who glory in their jurisdiction over others. These too would find themselves very unhappy on a planet where all are considered equal, where one entrusted with authority over others in an educational or community capacity must be the most humble servant among his fellowmen. This, of course, demands a condition of the heart, a love such as comparatively few on Earth have grown into. One cannot learn this lesson through books, only through living. And Earth is where Man is given the opportunity to learn such living, among others who are learning the same lessons.

On Earth there are those who feel a possessiveness over other members of their families, or perhaps of friends or acquaintances. Often such people feel it is entirely within their rights to dictate the acts and even the thoughts of others. People on Venus, on the other hand, never take such an attitude. They recognize each person's inherent freedom, granted by the Creator, and although one may not think or act in accordance with another's ideas, humility and compassion compel individuals to permit all others the liberty of their divine birthright.

The humble man sees all persons as equals, children of the same Creator, breathing the same breath of life, enjoying food from the same earth, sustained by the same sunshine and by the light of the same moon. Each person is born for a purpose of serving, as well as learning. No one can perfectly fill another's position because each has traveled his own path along which he has arrived at the present with its apparent condition.

The people on other planets are doing the same as we. They too are traveling the pathway of life, learning lessons every day.

At times they discover that they have not built a foundation with which to stand the stresses and strains put upon the average man by our way of life. These have to return to their planet, and, if through the passing of time they reach the point where they must learn through experience the lessons of our world, they will have to be born here in order to build a foundation through which they may learn them. Others, who have grown sufficiently in understanding and control of themselves, are able to meet the problems of everyday life on Earth in a calm manner without being overcome by them.

Many of the meetings I have had with our visitors have dealt mostly with my own problems and possible solutions. While they never advise a fellowman, they have an inexplicable ability of passing thoughts to another in such a way that he believes them to be his own. Thus he is free to accept and follow them, or discard them without the thought that someone else advised him. I had to learn this myself as I carefully studied my thoughts and acts following meetings with them. Often I found myself going exactly opposite to thoughts that I had received, all because I had not understood. It takes considerable schooling of oneself in this respect, and I still have a long way to go before I have mastered this lesson.

Another thing I have noticed about the space visitors, they love fun, singing, dancing, sports of all kinds, movies and educational programs on instruments comparable to our radio and TV. Yet they are always quiet. They do not talk a lot because, as they have explained, much effort is expended in talking. A great percentage of everyday talk on Earth is idle waste of time that enervates not only the speaker but others in his presence. Many people talk incessantly and loudly only because of nervous energy which they do not understand. Few people on our planet understand themselves, or have ever taken the time, thought and effort to gain such understanding. If we are to grow as we should, preparing ourselves for life in another classroom of the Cosmos, we will have to begin taking more interest in understanding our thoughts and their effects upon us as well as others, turning our minds toward the source of these thoughts and the reasons we allow them to possess us. In reality, we should be the masters of our thoughts, yet how many of us are?

I have been asked many times to describe the way of life on other planets, their homes, their interests, detailed conditions of all kinds. This is as impossible as it would be to describe the people and conditions in the entire world after one has met only a mere handful of people.

Through the years I have met individuals from many of our neighboring planets. From their personal appearances I could not tell any of them from ordinary Earthmen. Most of those whom I have met have come from Venus, so I have been told more about that planet than the others. On each planet a planetary language is spoken, rather than many languages as on Earth. Yet that of each planet differs from all others. So when space travelers visit from one planet to another, they take the interest and effort to learn the language spoken in the world they are to visit. Even so, this is not so difficult as coming to Earth and having to learn many languages if they hope to travel from one country to another. All planets have land masses, islands, continents and bodies of water, much like ours. Some have more water than others, but water must be present to support atmosphere and life.

Education on our neighboring planets begins at birth. A newborn child is observed lovingly and carefully to learn its thought patterns and its natural interests. This does not mean that it has the privilege of ruling the home, as so often occurs on Earth! From the beginning a child is taught the value and rewards of humility, consideration for others and the indescribable joy of loving and being loved. He is taught that his natural beauty and talents are gifts from the Creator to be used as a privilege.

Our neighbors in space have certain principles by which to live. These are the foundation upon which a child's life is based, and upon which adults, for the most part, strive to adhere. These are:

1. To desire no more than is actually needed for daily health and comfort.
2. To look upon all people as equals, without favoritism to any.

69

3. To watch and control their thoughts, keeping them universal at all times. This, with them as with us, is a great problem to which they keep ever alert. They do not always succeed, because they too have emotions which they have not entirely mastered. But when they catch themselves erring, those who have not turned into the detour of egotism immediately change to the universal aspect, looking upon their error as a lesson to be remembered and not to be repeated.

4. To appreciate and give thanks to every form for service rendered. This begins with each new day which they greet with pleasure and enthusiasm for opportunities it may present to serve the Creator.

As they have studied themselves, their thoughts and their impressions, they have learned to accept and act upon them in their purity rather than distorting them with biased reasoning as we are so prone to do. Thus the works of their hands express a beauty of natural radiation not found on Earth. Their stones, metals and minerals are no different from ours in this world, but their natural resonance is higher because of the absence of the negative attitudes so prevalent on Earth.

Homes in different parts of Venus are constructed for comfort and according to natural conditions, the same as they are here. There is a variety of architectual styles, as one would normally expect from a multitude of people. Their homes are no larger than is required for comfort and pleasure. Some families, because of their interests, prefer homes with lawns, flowers, swimming pools, etc., the same as we enjoy. There are others who prefer smaller quarters without so much responsibility. Accommodations are available for such prefences. One important difference their precepts of life have established from our Earthly ways, is their friendliness. One does not have to be invited to enjoy another's swimming pool or lawn and garden for instance, because all are considered friends and welcomed as such. The conveniences are not privately owned, but open for the pleasure of all.

As on Earth, businesses of various kinds are a necessity for the welfare and comfort of the people. Buildings must be constructed. Factories of all kinds are necessary to supply manufactured products. Farmers cultivate land to produce food. Shops, varying in size and style, accommodate the shopper. Trained workers keep public utilities and equipment in repair, since any man-made object is subject to flaws and breakdown.

The power they use is the same natural energy used in their ships; therefore, smoke and dirt are not produced, as is true of our power. Yet Nature has her storms there as here and there are few if any differences between dust particles of Venus and those of Earth.

They have solved the cleaning problem better than we have however. In each building—home, business, etc.—is built a magnetic suction system to draw floating particles of dust into a central container before they have an opportunity to settle. These containers are collected regularly, taken to a reclamation plant where the contents are processed to reclaim valuable minerals, much as fumes from our large factories and mills are trapped to extract usable elements for manufacturing by-products.

For the housewife, cooking is simple and easy. Most of the food is eaten in its natural state. That which they cook is quickly and simply prepared so as to retain vital minerals which would be washed away by the kind of soaking that is so often done by Earthly housewives, then quickly cooked with a penetrating ray. Similar equipment is now being developed in our world and will be put on the market for our homemakers.

I have not learned about the matter of dishwashing—which seems to be such an obstacle in the minds of many Earth people!

Venusians keep their clothes clean by use of a process similar to our ultra-sonic methods. By putting garments into a cabinet, they are cleaned better than by use of water or any of our solvents. The fabric is refreshed into its original state of newness through this method, thus increasing life and permitting it to retain its natural beauty. This process is used in cleaning all fabric, and takes only about three minutes. All homes, and public places like hotels, are equipped

71

with one or more of these cabinets, varying in size according to the need.

As on Earth, there are those creative men and women who delight in styling and making clothes. Some do this for the general public, others for their families and friends who do not share such interests or talents. They never allow their work to become a burden to them. This is because of their mental attitude and control over their thoughts. They have learned to enjoy thoroughly whatever they set themselves to do. We could do the same—if we wanted to, and would set ourselves toward this end. Admittedly, it is difficult, but not impossible.

Because of their excellent community transportation systems, and their desire not to possess more than they acutally need, few people own private vehicles. They realize, as many of our people are beginning to, that possessions can become the masters, with their owners being possessed and bound with extra cares, work and expenses.

True, they have robots to do much of the heavy work that once was done by manual labor. These have given the laborers more time for study and the pleasure of living. Still, it does take the mind of man to conceive and design machines of all kinds, and to maintain such equipment. Man, as he turns his thoughts into forms, becomes a creator.

Learning is a matter of a lifetime, never limited to a few short years in school. Their schools are edifices of beauty, within which is taught the science of living.

Many other sciences are also taught, with models depicting the history of their planet, civilizations that have come and gone, as well as history of other planets within our System, and systems beyond ours.

I was interested in the explanation they gave of the Garden of Eden as described in our Bible. This was a word picture of what results when Man permits his reason to separate him from an awareness of that eternal part of himself which we have named the "soul." The Cosmic man, unit of the Creative force and intelligence, builds the physical body and enables it to grow and express. So long as Man abides in the consciousness of this eternal part of himself, he never grows old, nor does he experience tensions or strains of any

72

kind. But when the reasoning mind, or personality ego, takes over, judgments enter and divisions are established which eventually lead to Man's downfall, and eventual destruction of that era of civilization.

The story of Adam and Eve is allegorical, depicting the history of mankind. When Man is aware of his true being, his lot is happiness, but when personal emotions—the "tempter" of greeds, envies, etc.—are allowed to rule him, he is taken out of his "Garden of Eden" into the world of hardships established by the ego.

The story of the Prodigal Son's return is a portrayal of man being humbled through hardships, turning again to an awareness of his true status as the child of the Infinite Creator, and the peace and joys that such awareness bring to their possessor.

Much teaching is done by means of systems similar to our radio and TV. Demonstrations are given of miniature solar systems in the process of being formed, while others are experiencing disintegration. Cosmic laws, as learned through observation with telescopic instruments on the planet as well as in their space travels, are taught with the aid of replicas built for use in their schools. Classes are not established by ages, but by interest of the people. No one is pushed beyond his interest, nor is anyone held back in his progress by a prevailing "average." This may all sound pointless to us who have grown accustomed to our system of education, but on a planet where interest is a stimulant for greater understanding of that which is limitless, no monotony or indifference is allowed to rule a person.

There are no separate churches, as we have them, for their day-by-day living incorporates what we might term their "religion." With their attitudes and understanding of Universal Laws, there can be no divisions as between religious teaching and daily living, for in the house of the Creator there is eternal blending of all things. One studies to learn that he might more fully live according to the will of the Infinite and thereby progress along the pathway of eternal life.

Little ones are taught in their homes, as well as in such public institutions. One never grows so old as to stop attending classes of instruction. Periodic travel on their planet and elsewhere through the Cosmos in their gigantic luxury space liners is enjoyed by every individual on Venus, regardless of age. They have learned well that, although one can learn much through study of records and miniature replicas, travel is a source of unending practical education which gives not only pleasure but lessons of lasting value, never forgotten.

People on Venus know no disease of mind or body, as they are free of tensions, such as are created by our personality divisions, likes and dislikes, and judgments of one kind or another. This was told in *Inside the Space Ships.** Many people have written to me, asking if the space people cannot give us information which would enable us to heal some of the most prevalent and cruel diseases being suffered by Earth's humanity.

This subject has been discussed on a number of occasions.

The human body, as we all know, is the most perfect machine ever created. It works, when allowed to do so, in perfect balance and harmony. No organ or part of the body takes an attitude that it is better than all other parts, or that it is being worked more than the others. Each performs its duty freely and happily, so long as the mind of the individaul permits such co-operation. The only exception is a deformity of some kind, which in many instances can be traced back to ignorance on the part of parents during prenatal development. Even then, the well-developed portions take on an extra responsibility in an effort to establish harmony and to rebuild the body into the perfect pattern set for it in the beginning.

Our scientists know this. They are learning the tremendous effect the mind has on the body and its functions. Yet people seldom realize how their tensions, their worries and emotions of all kinds affect their health. Our present social system has created conditions which build barriers for us to hurdle as we endeavor to fulfill demands made upon us. The patterns were set up long ago, but have become intensified during the years. Today people are dropping over from

*published as *Inside the Flying Saucers* by Paperback Library, Inc. (# 53-428, 60¢)

74

heart attacks and suffering from malignant diseases of several types. Respiratory diseases are on the increase, sometimes differing in symptoms and intensity of reactions. People are wearing glasses more than ever before, because of eye strains of many varieties.

Few people ever really take time to relax. In fact, I doubt that many people even know how to relax, not only the body but also the mind, for the conditions in the body are but reflections of mental tenseness. Our present state is not the result of today or yesterday alone, but the accumulation of patterns started years ago and multiplied by each individual thought and act through this time, until the patterns thus established affect not only humans but all forms on our earth.

Some of the space visitors who have no natural tensions in their way of life are affected by Earthly conditions, even by our atmosphere which we have so polluted during the past fifteen or twenty years.

Health is an individual problem. One cannot keep "burning the candle at both ends," with the brakes of tension applied most of the time, and hope to keep well. Many people have gone on like this for years, achieving a certain amount of what was considered success, only to be struck down and bed-ridden for weeks, months, or even years. Some have been wise enough to recognize their trouble and have learned to take things easy, without worrying or resentment of any kind. These often have recovered and lived long years, enjoying whatever the moment brought. I have myself known some such people who, while confined and forced to rest, learned to control their tempers, became aware of advance indications they were overstressing and building a tension and have thus been able to relax before another breakdown. It would not be necessary to experience such conditions if we would only begin to study ourselves, watch our thoughts and their effects upon ourselves and those around us, and then take time and make the effort toward relaxation. If only we would do this, we would find that in an amazingly short time, many things would change for the one who had made such an effort. If all of the people of the world would do so, there would be world-wide changes beyond anyone's expectation. Some will be able to master the art of relaxation much more quickly than others. For all it will mean patience and persistence. But the rewards will be gratifying to any who will make the effort.

A warning, however. One cannot achieve relaxation through a strong determination that serves more to tighten than to loosen. True relaxation is found through happiness—happy thoughts are powerful, for happiness frees.

These are the reasons given by our interplanetary visitors for being unable to help us in our health problems more than they have. Yet they have continuously sent us thoughts of happiness, free of all condemnation. Again, I must repeat that they look upon us as younger brothers whom they love dearly, but whom they know must solve their own problems in order to learn the lessons well. When we have learned to relax mentally, we will also become more receptive to their thoughts of help. A tense mind is incapable of receptivity to much of anything but its own thoughts.

As Ruskin said: "Make yourself nests of pleasant thoughts." If you do, you will find the way made easier. Do as the space people do, release your own mistakes—everyone makes them—learn the lessons they have for you so that you do not repeat them, but let them go.

Another important factor in the health of our neighbors on other planets is their custom of regular exercise to keep the body supple. They look upon their bodies as beautiful temples of divine creation which should be cared for with love and faithfulness. Dancing, swimming, sports of all kinds are indulged in with happiness, for sheer pleasure. They enjoy rhythm and strive to keep their bodies expressing their natural rhythm, thus maintaining a healthful state. They never make exercise a labor, for that would create tensions. Happiness and joyous expression alone can accomplish relaxation through exercise.

I have never been on another planet, not even on our moon. All I can tell is what has been given to me by those of other planets who have honored me with their visits. Through the years I have grown in understanding their concept of the Creator as expressed through all forms, and man as an *eternal* manifestation. It is through this realization that

76

they have grown in their ability to forget the past and live for the present. They have conscious perception which does not permit them to sit among any group of people without a thought of blessing. For, although the forms may be what we have named "human," those of higher understanding see them not merely as people, but as the Divine Intelligence in a living state with which they can find no fault.

People on Venus live hundreds of years in a single life span, then go through the experience we have named "death." To them it is but a moving out of one house that has served them well into another new house. The minerals of the body, having originated from their planet, are returned once again to the planet. Rather than mourning for the loss of a loved one, as is the custom on Earth, people on Venus rejoice in their loved one's opportunity to express through a new home somewhere in the Father's house of many mansions. Since there is no feeling of possession of one for another, there is no suffering due to separation, for the true love as understood by them knows no separation of any kind.

To say that I have grown to the place where I live as they do would not be true. But since man is eternal, each successful effort takes me a step farther along the path of progress. It requires constant effort, with eternity in which to succeed. The wise man knows that only as he learns to live moment by moment will progress be his; for it is always the present. The past is gone and cannot be changed regardless how one might like to change it. The future can never be reached, not even the coming moment. When it arrives, it is the present.

These are the lessons Earth's inhabitants are to learn. No one can do it for them, any more than one man can eat for another and both reap benefits. Growth and progress are individual matters. The way may be pointed, but each must travel it for himself. He may choose to travel the main highways, meeting and mastering the lessons brought by each moment, or he may choose detours. The choice lies with each one alone.

Nothing that the space travelers have told us is new. Their wisdom has been with us for centuries. In the past we have chosen to ignore it, giving excuses of one kind or another.

77

They are but reminding us and in simple, understandable language, again showing us the way of a life of peace and happiness which is the Father's will for all of His children, wherever they may be throughout the vastness of infinity in His house of many mansions . . . a life of eternal blend, without divisions, as is expressed throughout Nature in all of her phases. Once we accept Nature as our teacher, many "mysteries" will be revealed to us in all of their simplicity.

As to which planets the space people consider higher or lower, they make no such distinctions. Each is a classroom of the Cosmos in which specific lessons can be learned better than elsewhere. Yet all lessons are important in a complete life. It is only on Earth that we make divisions of higher or lower, better or worse.

Mars, as I understand, is highly developed in science and manufacturing. But there, as on Venus, there is no bondage.

When we depict Saturn with the symbol of scales, we are correct, for she is the planet of balance in many ways. In relation to the system, she serves as a balance between the planets, the sun, and the asteroid belts.

Venus, of course, is the planet on which lessons in love and compassion predominate, to be used as the foundation upon which all human attitudes and acts are based.

I was not given specific information regarding other planets, but if we of Earth can learn to live a little more like the Venusians in their feelings toward one another; grow scientifically for the welfare of all, as the Martians; and gain more balance between play and relaxation and work as the Saturnians; we will find ourselves very well occupied. If we can or will make such endeavors, the history of our world will take a turn and we will in time be eligible to take our place in the household of our system.

10. THE BIBLE AND THE UFO

(All references are to the King James Version)

MANY PEOPLE who have read my first two books, *Flying Saucers Have Landed* and *Inside the Space Ships,** have written to ask why, if people are living on other planets, are they not mentioned in the Scriptures? I have conducted quite a bit of research into this subject, as the space people have told me many times of their visitations in Bibical times.

As a student of philosophy and science for many years, I have taught that the other planets were inhabited. This was long before I had seen a "flying saucer" or had had the pleasure of personal contacts with their occupants. My meetings with these people should not be considered such an unusual thing, as many others have experienced the same type of contacts. (I am not referring to the many claiming psychic contacts. The people I am referring to have not publizied their experiences.) These other contacts are known to various governments of the world, and due to the ridiculous light in which the "saucers" find themselves at present, their identities are being kept quiet. In the meantime they are studying and preparing for the day when they will be unveiled to the world. They will begin teaching the knowledge they have acquired to the masses, who will suddenly awake and find that they have been following the false ideas built up over the centuries and hidden by their own closed minds.

Careful research of the Bible brings to light many reports of the visitors. In fact, a minister told me that he had found over 350 such references. Not only our Bible but other great records mention the coming of the visitors. Most of the people who wrote asking why they were not mentioned were simply uninformed as to the actual records. It is with this idea in mind that I will attempt to show how the visitors from space are mentioned in the Bible and that it was common practice for space people to offer guidance to the peoples of the world in ancient times, just as they are attempting to do now.

One of the first verses brought to mind at this time is found

*published as *Inside the Flying Saucers* by Paperback Library, Inc. (# 53-428, 60¢)

in Hebrews 1:2. "[God] Hath in these last days spoken unto us by his Son, whom he hath appointed heir of all things, by whom also he made the worlds." This is a definite reference to more than one world. A similar concept is shown in Hebrews 11:3: "Through faith we understand that the worlds were framed by the word of God, so that things which are seen were not made of things which do appear." Here again we find another reference to more than one world. Nothing was said about these worlds being inhabited but it is proof that other worlds were known in Biblical times.

These people in Biblical times were aware that the worlds were "made of things that do not appear." These worlds came out of the invisible into the visible—or from cause to effect. This idea coincides with the most advanced conceptions of today in regard to the origin of the solar systems.

In the Gospel of St. John 14:2 we read: "In my father's house are many mansions: If it were not so, I would have told you. I go to prepare a place for you." This shows clearly that if we evolve enough we can go to another world and live just as He stated He was going to do. This is shown in the next verse (John 14:3): "And if I go and prepare a place for you, I will come again, and receive you unto myself; that where I am, there ye may be also."

It is illogical to believe that Christ was the only inhabitant of His world. His planet must have had millions of happy people who were considered angels when they periodically traveled to Earth.

It is taught that Jesus was taken up bodily into heaven and this alone is proof that somewhere out there exists a planet capable of supporting life. Christ Himself gave ample evidence that He came from another world. In St. John 8:23 we find: "And He said unto them, Ye are from beneath; I am from above: ye are of this world; I am not of this world." This shows we are of this world and are born from it. He was born of this world but was not from it. He came here from another. This is one of the better references referring to a being on a higher planet volunteering to be born here on earth; this for the express purpose of guiding and helping those who are still climbing the ladder of spiritual evolution.

We are taught in the Bible that we can become like Christ

and even do greater things than He. We are taught that He was the firstborn of many brethren and that some day many of us can attain equal status with Christ. (Rom. 8:29.)

This is in full accord with the statements of the space visitors where they said the earth was like the first grade of a grade-school. As we progress higher and higher we move up through the planets as one going from the first to second and third grades and so on. We climb from grade to grade and from planet to planet.

At times there are those who desire to return to earth to help those who are still climbing here. This is much like our sending missionaries to some foreign country. Some would choose to be born here as Jesus was. Others choose to come here in ships and live here as one of us. Many hundreds are doing that today.

The Bible has other direct evidence that other worlds are inhabited. Genesis 6:2 and 6:4 describes sons of God who "came in unto the daughters of men, and they bare children to them, the same became mighty men which were of old, men of renown."

These sons of God were evidently enough like human men of earth to give children to the Earthwomen of that time. They were flesh and blood like ourselves. I am sure that no one would claim that spirits or spirit angels came down and had relations with these women. They must have been as human as you or I This is definite proof that other planets are inhabited and have been for a long time.

The Biblical description of angels is very clear. They look exactly like men of Earth. They are just like us except that they didn't participate in the Fall of Man. Positive proof of their looks is given in the Epistle to the Hebrews where we find we can entertain them without being aware they are angels. (Heb. 13:2.)

We have heard much about spacemen and women being on Earth. This seems fantastic and laughable to many because of what they have been taught from childhood. But if some have entertained strangers and didn't know they were angels, then who is to say that these men and women are not among us now as they were in olden times. You yourself may have entertained them or met them on the streets, as many have, including myself. Many people are aware of the identity of these visitors; many are not. If we believe that history repeats itself, then why not Biblical history as well?

How many times have the flying saucers been reported leaving the mother ship, scouting over the earth and then returning to the ship? A perfect description of this type of activity is found in Isaiah 60:8. "Who are these that fly as a cloud, and as the doves to their windows?" Does this not sound like flying saucers being gathered in by a mother ship? Phraseology in those days was different from today, and 500 years from now it will be different again, but there is always a basic principle by which we can identify similar happenings.

The first chapter of Ezekiel is an amazing story of phenomena that follows the usual UFO reports too exactly to be mere coincidence. In the fourth verse we find a machine described as like a "whirlwind" coming out of the north with a great amber cloud of fire around it. Inside were four living creatures who looked like men. (Ezek. 1:5.)

At this point I would like to comment upon an odd characteristic of these ancient writings. In the original manuscripts no punctuation was used and no separations were placed between words and sentences. Furthermore no divisions into verses or chapters appeared. All this was added later by the revisors and translators. Scholars have commented upon the fact that Ezekiel had a habit of jumping about in his writings. This makes it hard to separate the descriptions of the living beings and the ships. In many cases a verse describing the men is followed by one referring to the ship and the very next verse refers to the men again. With this in mind let us go on.

Verse 5 just stated that creatures looking like men were inside the ship which was glowing very brightly. Verse 6 says "every one had four faces and every one had four wings." Obviously if the beings had four faces and four wings they wouldn't look like men. Verse 6 does not describe the men but rather the ships themselves. This is made plain in other translations of the Bible. Some of these even describe the ships as disks.

The ancient writers of that day had no words to describe

directions as we do. For example they referred to north, south, east, and west, as the four corners of the world. In verse 6 the ships are described as being round and facing in all directions by the use of the terms "every one had four faces" and four wings, or, in other words, faced in four directions at the same time. To add to the difficulty of understanding these verses, the next verse jumps back to a description of the men. We find they had straight feet like us but were wearing strange shoes made of calf-hide that was brass-colored and were obviously some type of sandal or moccasin.

Verse 8 makes it clear that they were guided by the hands of men or had men as pilots. In verse 9 is described a characteristic of modern-day "saucers." They "turned not when they went; they every one went straight forward." The ancient writer describes the character of the men and the determination showing in their faces by saying they have the strength of a lion, the steadfastness of an ox and the agility of an eagle. Obviously these beings could not look like men if they looked like animals. The writer of this description used symbolism just as we might in saying someone has a bulldog jaw or a Roman nose. Verse 12 makes it obvious that the faces in verse 11 were part of the ship itself and not faces of the men. So we see that the term "face" is used in referring both to the ship and to the men. Most of the confusion probably arose in translation as the translators themselves were trying to interpret something of which they were in complete ignorance. No doubt if we could have understood the language and read it as it was originally meant to be, we would understand exactly what the writer tried to convey and the confusion in terms would have been avoided.

These flying machines landed; and what then transpired is related in verses 15 through 28. At rest the machines were the color of beryl. All four were made alike and were constructed "as it were a wheel in the middle of a wheel." Verse 17 again asserts they were round and changed directions without turning. Verse 18 describes the high ring around the dome and even goes so far as to describe four portholes. These verses are a very accurate description of the three-ball-landing-gear type of saucer as seen through the eyes of Ezekiel.

Under the flange of the scout type craft are three revolving gears of metal as reported many times before. Not only do they give gyroscopic stabilization but they serve as generators of the tremendous electrostatic charge that is built up and stored in the Van de Graaff accumulators that are inside the three-ball landing gear. An observer of these "wheels within a wheel" would describe them exactly as Ezekiel did.

Verses 19 and 20 make it very plain that the men rode inside the ships and had full control over the movements at all times. The rest of the chapter describes the "contact" and when Ezekiel heard a man speak to him out of the ship he fell on his face and attributed the strange machine and happenings to angels and God. Ezekiel was in awe of the many changing colors of the craft's force field and describes them fully in verses 22 through 28. His reaction was very much like the reaction of so many today. When he stumbled across something he didn't understand he attributed it to God or the unknown and failed to realize that he was only contacting other human beings from another world.

Jeremiah the prophet referred to flying chariots appearing as clouds. (Jer. 4:13.) Many times since the advent of flying saucers, people have reported seeing in the daytime what appeared to be a cloud. Suddenly, from inside the cloud, a saucer would dart out and the cloud would slowly evaporate and disappear. This phenomena is caused by the force field of the craft itself. It causes the air to condense and form a cloud. This cloud has frequently been observed either around the ship or just above it.

The children of Israel were led at night by a pillar of fire and by day with a cloud. (Exod. 13:21) When they were pursued by the Egyptians it is recorded that this cloud and pillar of fire "troubled" the pursuers as they were unfamiliar with such phenomena.

Notice the word "Lord" used in Exodus, chapter 13 and 14. I would like to make it clear that ever since we can remember, man has been taught by various religious groups that the earth was the only inhabited place where man dwelled. Everything above the earth—or the sky—was the dwelling place of gods, angels and lords. Anything these people observed coming to earth from above—since they had no such means of travel themselves—was either gods, angels, or lords.

A good example of not only a contact but a ride also is recorded in the Second Book of Kings "And it came to pass, as they still went on, and talked, that, behold, there appeared a chariot of fire, and horses of fire, and parted them both asunder; and Elijah went up by a whirlwind into heaven." (II Kings 2:11.)

First the fiery chariot was seen—most saucer reports described the ship as surrounded by an orange or amber fireball effect—and the tremendous power is symbolized by horses of fire. When it came close it could be felt as the wind of a whirlwind.

Elijah was considered to be a man of God and perhaps he was a spaceman who upon finding his work finished in that locality decided to leave and go to others. He was aware that he would be taken up and had promised his cloak of authority to Elisha when he left. So this event did not take him by surprise. At any event it was men like himself that took Elijah up from the earth and took him to another point on it. He didn't go away from the earth at that time for we find that a few years later (II Chron. 21:12), Elijah, writing from another area, condemned Jehoram for departing from the teachings of his father and for slaying all his relatives who might jeopardize his throne. Scholars agree that this was over ten years (at least) from the time Elijah had been caught up. Elijah was returned to earth at another place to teach these other people what he had learned. This could be the answer to some of our present-day disappearances that so many have wondered about. Perhaps some of these people were "visitors" living among us who decided to go back to their own planet and simply disappeared from our midst by way of space ships sent to gather them.

Moses frequently conversed with beings speaking out of a ball of fire or out of a glowing cloud. (Exod. 33:9.) Many times a spaceman in a space ship came down in front of the tabernacle and talked to Moses. The following verse shows that all the people witnessed this event.

A similar event is recorded in Psalm 99 where we find "He spake unto them in the cloudy pillar: they kept his testimonies, and the ordinance that he gave them." (Ps. 99:7.) Notice throughout the Bible that when Earthmen have gotten too far out of line, these messengers, or spacemen in their space ships, have come down and talked to the leaders or to some of the community. Each time they would give them some of the Universal Laws and try to guide them in correcting their ways. Notice that they only informed them how to overcome their difficulties. The people had to accept and change their own ways. If they refused and brought trouble upon themselves, they could blame no one else for what happened.

In Luke, Chapter 9, verses 34 and 35, we find an account of a ship in a cloud and a voice coming out of the cloud. The disciples were afraid when the ship approached, just as many people today are afraid when a similar incident occurs. The fact that a voice came from the ship is further proof of instructions given by spacepeople to the people of earth.

Acts 1:9 is an account of Christ's ascension. This was after the resurrection and Christ had appeared in His physical body over a period of 40 days. We have always been taught that He ascended in His physical body. When He entered the space ship, the "cloud received Him out of their sight." The next two verses show there were witnesses to the event. Also, there is the promise that this same Jesus will return in like manner from heaven—or the sky. This covers this aspect pretty well although there are many more references to this particular point.

We will now try to clarify the statement by Orthon in *Inside the Space Ships*,* pages 237 and 238: "I call your attention to a record contained within your own Holy Writ. If you study it carefully, you will notice that the span of life on earth began to decrease when the cloudy formation lessened and men for the first time saw the stars out in space." This refers to what we now call firmament. Now I will confirm his statement proving they know more about the Bible than we do.

Genesis 9:29 shows that Noah lived nine hundred and fifty

*published as *Inside the Flying Saucers* by Paperback Library, Inc. (# 53-428, 60¢)

years. The first Biblical account of man seeing the stars is found in Genesis 15:5 where Abram (Abraham) is told to look to the heavens and count the stars. We are not sure just when the perpetual clouds ceased to cover the earth. We know most of the moisture contained in these clouds fell as rain during the flood of Noah. After the flood, the skies gradually cleared and sometime in between the time of Noah and Abraham, stars were seen for the first time. When the cloud cover disappeared the deadly cosmic rays spread upon the earth and Man's life span decreased very rapidly. Abraham died at the age of 175 years. (Gen. 25:7, 8.)

In tracing the family tree from Noah to Abraham we find eleven generations. During these generations the life span dropped from Noah's 950 years to Abraham's 175 years— and since then to an average of 65 years.

It is amazing that the space people are able to recall those days and tell us what is happening and why, as they have in *Flying Saucers Have Landed* and *Inside the Space Ships*. My first two books carried the full story of what is really taking place.

One of my correspondents, who is a Biblical student, sent me the following information which may be of some help to the public in general. I have not personally checked this however. "The prophetic depictions of the wheels were made in 595 B.C. Later, John the Revelator was apparently inspired to write further details in connection with the 'living creatures,' in 96 A.D. Regarding the phenomena of 'power blasts' (seemingly as manifested by a form of cosmic or nuclear energy) these accounts were recorded from approximately 1491 B.C. to 712 B.C."

These accounts are found throughout the Bible.

In these days we are passing through a stage of life where the religious leaders of this world should take very serious note. We have been taught by these leaders, since man can remember, that Jesus was born of flesh and blood like any Earthling. We are taught that He took that body to heaven (or the sky, as the sky was always referred to as heaven in those days).

A few years ago we were told that the Holy Church proclaimed that Mary, the mother of Jesus, was taken up the same way. Many churches teach that both Elijah and Enoch were caught up alive into heaven also. These people went alive to some other planet where they apparently were able to live in comfort.

All of this proves that when we get space ships, as the spacemen do, we should be able to travel to their planets and continue to live there. We have been taught this in our religious thought. We uphold the statement made by Jesus of the "many mansions." We also have the prayer, "Thy will be done on earth as it is in heaven." How are we to obey this command unless someone from "heaven" comes down to instruct us? All these things have been prophesied to us and we have been told they would take place, things such as strange happenings in the skies. These things are being fulfilled, are they not?

What is our ministry going to do? Are they going to tell us they have been teaching us a fairy story all the time? Or are they going to admit that these things are true now, that what they have been teaching all this time was the truth and today we have the manifestation of that truth. It is quite important that they do consider this, since the Bible mentions so many such manifestations in the early times.

If this happens it will mean that these space ships, known as flying saucers, do support our teachings and do support the records of the Bible. If we are to accept the Bible and the teachings of the ministry as the truth, then now is the time to prove them to be. These appearances of flying saucers are fulfilling prophecy. Besides, we must admit—there is no use fooling ourselves—our younger generation is not going to fill our churches as the older generation has. This is especially true since every government in the world is endeavoring to build satellites to send into outer space. I feel that within a comparatively short time we will be traveling through space to another planet in one of our own ships.

Each time we venture farther into space, these youngsters who are space-minded—and there are millions of them—will be seeing this development of outer space as a vast contrast to the teachings they have been receiving from the spiritual side. Unless the spiritual leaders of today can blend with the advancement of man into space, by 1970 they will find their churches empty and themselves out of a job. These youngsters of today will see facts and reality and will follow them. They are so inclined right now.

We are in those days. "For we wrestle not against flesh and blood, but against principalities, against powers, against the rulers of the darkness of this world, against spiritual wickedness in high places." (Eph. 6:12.)

Apply this to the world today and what have you? We can see what is actually happening and whether the prophecies are actually being fulfilled. This should not cause any fear; this should be accepted with understanding, an admission of things that are present.

The Bible states that in the latter days men's hearts shall fail them for fear. (Luke 21:26.) I don't want to be a preacher in the sense of preaching, but I cannot ignore the truth. Notice how people all over the world are dying of heart failure today. Just as the prophecy foretold. Why? Because upon the earth we find the nations perplexed and in distress. We find the sea and the waves roaring. (Luke 21:25.) We are having earthquakes and tidal waves such as the world has never seen before. We have had as many major earthquakes in fourteen weeks as is normal in two and one-half years. (Luke 21:11.) Let us wake up. Let us humble our ego a little and we might see clearly what is taking place.

The saucers are not here to harm or frighten anyone. They have injured no one, although they have been accused by those who do not understand their purpose. They have not committed hostile acts against our planes or kidnapped their crews. Some may have been taken—just as Elijah was—and later returned to teach what they know. Maybe this is yet to come and those who have vanished will be returning with such messages—if we do not put them in the psycho wards.

Could it be that we are the guilty ones? Captain Ruppelt's book admitted that our military men have shot at them. If these objects are what the Air Force claims, why shoot? If they are interplanetary space ships, why shoot? In the latter case, anyone with a technology great enough to travel space could certainly shoot back. The fact they haven't proves conclusively that these visitors are friendly and have no desire for the conquest of our planet. If they had desired to conquer us, we would have been entirely unable to defend ourselves. We could never exceed their scientific ability, and most certainly we could never catch up to them in any of the best rockets or planes we have.

They have never shown any type of hostility toward us. Since everything that comes from the sky (or heaven) has always been considered an angel, god or lord, then are we not shooting at angels? Does not this fulfill the Biblical prophecy that in the last days the nations of Earth will resist the angels coming from heaven to help us in our time of need? Remember, angels were always described as normal men. Nowhere does the Bible say angels have wings. Genesis 18:2 describes three angels who appeared unto Abraham, as looking exactly like three men. In many Biblical cases we find angels who walked along a road with people, partook of their food or lodging and later revealed themselves as angels instead of the ordinary men they looked. (Heb. 13:2; Luke 16:5; etc.)

Who is to say that these people from other planets are not being sent here as they were in earlier days? Every time Man gets into trouble they seem to appear and instruct him on how to overcome his troubles. If he listens he usually gets out of trouble with a minimum of effort or ill effect but if he ignores the advice, he receives just what he has earned. What greater trouble could the world be in, than that in which it finds itself right now?

Many people want to know if the space people are Christians. I would say they are better Christians than we are. We have never believed in the teachings of Jesus. We have rehearsed them and that is all. We have done this in order to keep the "Christian" label and His name before the people. But this is all. Anything a man believes, he lives, and we have never lived Christ's teachings.

Had we lived the teachings of Christ we would not have the pains, aches, sorrows or the threat of annihilation hanging over us today. If His teachings were applied to our everyday living, these conditions would not be present. A virtual heaven on earth would have been established.

Every now and then we rehearse Christ's teachings—on Sunday, Christmas, Easter—then we go right out and forget all about them until the next time we are reminded. We have never taken hold of them to the point of living them. Now again we find the messengers are warning us.

When I asked the "boys," as I stated in *Inside the Space Ships,** "If we should shoot you down or get you in the sights of our guns so we could shoot you down, would you defend yourself with the power you have?" they answered, "No. We would have to die, because we could not take advantage of our brothers who do not understand." Did not Jesus say the same thing when He was on the cross? "Father, forgive them for they know not what they do." We would have asked for revenge.

Let me emphasize this one point. I do not know of any man in any government who has not had some religious training, who does not pay respect to some Supreme Being, whatever his understanding may be. What does a man like that think about when he shoots at these people coming our way? If he believes his Bible and religious training, then he knows that angels have come from heaven to guide men and that they are to come again in the last days. He knows they have to return, if they ever left, to fulfill prophecy. Then is he not challenging the hand of God in shooting at them? Why try to destroy the messengers sent to aid us at this time? If we are going to claim ourselves as Christians, then let us follow Christian law instead of shooting at those who might be our very saviors.

Captain Ruppelt tells of instances when we have fired upon UFOs. While he does not refer to many cases, they have been shot at many times. According to some rumors, some of these ships have been brought down and lives sacrificed because of our ignorance.

Let us re-examine the whole situation in the light of God's own intelligence, the light of the true Christian—not that of a Christian in name alone. We will then understand the days we are living in and what we must be prepared for. When we do that we will be doing good for ourselves and serving our Creator and purpose as well. Then and only then can we consider ourselves as true Christians.

*published as *Inside the Flying Saucers* by Paperback Library, Inc. (# 53-428, 60¢)

These people are coming our way to help those who wish to know the truth. Let us not ignore them. Let us learn all we can so that we may be saved—if any saving is to be done. This means too that by saving humanity, this truth saves religion and also saves the church.

By promoting a friendly feeling toward these people from the heavens, we shall welcome them into our midst and our homes can be honored with their presence. As it states in Hebrews 13:2, "Be not forgetful to entertain strangers; for thereby some have entertained angels unawares." Many have undoubtedly done so already—many may have knowingly entertained them—but we can all entertain them when we develop the right attitude toward them.

Let us not be ashamed of Christ's teachings. Let us preach them, live them, and bring the knowledge of them closer to the hearts of every man. Not from an earthly angle, not from a church or denominational angle, but rather from a universal or cosmic angle. Did not Jesus say, "And other sheep I have, which are not of this fold: them also I must bring, and they shall hear my voice; and there shall be one fold, and one shepherd"? (John 10:16.)

The Bible gives positive evidence that the worlds were created expressly to be inhabited. Life is not an accident of nature. Isaiah 45:18 reads: "For thus saith the Lord that created the heavens; God himself that formed the earth and made it, he created it not in vain, he formed it to be inhabited: I am the Lord and there is none else." It is reasonable to assume that if God created this world to be inhabited, He must have created the others to be inhabited also.

The Bible backs up my previous statement that others not of this world are living among us. It is found in John 17:14 as follows: "I have given them thy word; and the world hath hated them, because they are not of this world, even as I am not of this world." Verse 16 repeats the statement. Some believe these verses refer to the apostles themselves and not to space people living among us. It is easy to see this is not the case, as Jesus, who is speaking, makes it a point to say "even as I am not of this world." This can mean the apostles themselves were born here from another world for the express purpose of working with Jesus. They could have been some of those who are born here with a partial or total loss of memory of previous experiences.

Even the mother ship is referred to in the Bible as a "flying roll." (Zech. 5:1-2.) The only common thing in that day and age that could be compared to a cigar-shaped spacecraft was a roll of parchment. In Zechariah 6:1 we find reference to four chariots that come out from between two mountains. Could these be the same as the chariots of Jeremiah 4:13? Here we find them coming as clouds, with chariots like the whirlwind and horses swifter than eagles. The reference to eagles and clouds shows that the chariots were flying.

It might be well at this time to comment upon the cherub of the Bible. The strange flying machines that Ezekiel saw, as described previously, were cherubs. These are thought to be some type of angel by some scholars of the Bible; however, they are used as a means of transportation in several instances showing they are ships of some kind. The cherub of Ezekiel remains a saucer.

Another example of a cherub is found in II Samuel 22:11: "And he rode upon a cherub, and did fly: and he was seen upon the wings of the wind." A parallel instance is recorded in Psalms 18:10. Here David calls upon the Lord for help and the Lord arrives on a cherub: "And he rode upon a cherub, and did fly; yea, he did fly upon the wings of the wind." The characteristic cloud of fire accompanies him.

Evidently the early church came to believe the cherub was an angel because it was described as flying on wings. They had no knowledge of the nature of the space travelers and assumed that the ships were fire-breathing animals of some sort. They couldn't conceive of mechanical constructions made to navigate the heavens. I imagine the automobile would have been described as another type of angel or cherub, or perhaps as a demon or devil.

The idea of angels having wings growing out of their shoulders and wearing long white robes, was instilled in the minds of present-day people by the great artists who pictured them as such. The Bible has always described them as ordinary men from other worlds.

It is affirmed that we can become like the space visitors if we so desire. Psalms 82:6 and John 10:34 both state: "ye are gods." So, we have the potential to climb back from where we have fallen. Let us strive mightily for the fulfillment of that destiny.

11. METAPHYSICS, PSYCHISM, RELIGION

BECAUSE THERE is so much confusion existing today in the minds of people who are seeking better understanding of themselves, the purpose of life in this world and factual information regarding people from other planets, it seems appropriate to give the definitions of several words that are commonly being misused today. These are words that have come into use in relation to the space travelers; but, in the sense in which they are being used, they have no place whatever.

If the reader will study carefully the definitions given below, he will quickly see that originally, and in their true essence, each of these words implies a seeking for understanding of the cause behind the manifested form.

The words *psyche* and *psychic* pertain to the human mind or soul, the sense mind that is so filled with confusion and divisions. *Psychic* denotes certain abnormal and obscure mental phenomena such as hypnotism, occultism, etc.

Occult is a word used to denote things hidden from the eye of understanding. Things mysterious, invisible, secret, undetected, etc., such as the *occult* qualities of matter. During the middle ages the occult sciences were what we now popularly call the physical and natural sciences—chemistry, physics, astronomy, etc.

Occultism itself is the investigation of mysterious things—the name given to a system of theosophy practiced in the East. Its adepts claim to be able to produce seemingly miraculous effects by purely natural means.

Theosophy, or wisdom concerning God, was the insight into the character and purposes of the divine mind, or knowledge of divine things. Specifically it was a system of religion based on the notion that a knowledge of divine things is gained by ecstasy, direct intuition, or special revelation.

Philosophy, as it is understood today, may be defined as the universal science which aims at an explanation of all the phenomena of the universe by ultimate causes. When applied to any particular department of knowledge, it denotes the collection of general laws or principles under which all the subordinate phenomena or facts related to that subject are comprised.

An area of great confusion exists concerning the word *metaphysics.* The so-called metaphysicians of today are not working with metaphysics at all. They have manufactured a pseudo-religious idea that in actuality is not at all related to any of the true metaphysical ideas. Metaphysics is the science of first or ultimate principles behind the explanation of all phenomena, philosophy in general. The philosophy of mind, *psychology,* or the science of mental phenomena, is a branch of metaphysics.

A little thought on the subject will quickly show one that present-day psychism, compared with the real meaning as given above, is nothing more than a perversion of the true science of the occult, metaphysics, etc. One cannot gain an understanding of any of these sciences overnight. It takes a lifetime of study and living to accomplish such knowledge. The real student never seeks publicity but lives quietly, studying and applying that which he learns. Such students never see any division between the invisible cause and the physical form. They realize that neither could be without the other; that an external blend makes the whole possible.

As he studies in this manner, the sincere seeker is often capable of observing pattern forms which culminate in definite events. Throughout the history of world events, certain patterns have been repeated time after time. The student realizes that, without intervention by other conditions, these patterns can and will work out again as time progresses. Because there is that unpredictable something about both Man and Nature, accurate prophecy cannot be made, especially as to a time and place for the complete and perfect working out of a form pattern. For these reasons, a wise man never gives dire warning of events to come, nor does he make definite promises when the unforeseeable may enter and change the course of events.

Compare, then, many of our present-day psychics, who claim to have attained overnight the power and understanding with which to prophesy, and who make personal promises to any and all—via, they say, communication with the space people. Physical or spirits, they care not. Their information for the most part is received through the Ouija board, automatic writing, trance, or invisible people "talking" into their minds.

By such methods promises have been made from time to time of mass landings by space people planning to take over control of Earth and her inhabitants. One man has declared himself to be the one chosen to become ruler of the world when this takes place. Nothing could be further from the truth!

The Brothers have no intention of taking over anybody. To the best of my knowledge, no Earthman has been appointed to act as their sole representative. True, many have volunteered their services, but not one has been accepted above all others.

In Europe I encountered reports of two Ashtars, totally different in character, but each claiming supreme command over large numbers of space travelers.

From such dubious sources have come promises of personal contacts, sometimes even with specific dates and instructions as to time and place. I have yet to hear of any of these promises being fulfilled. Many people have been promised rides in space ships and were sadly disillusioned when the trips did not occur. Warnings of tragic events to take place, with promises to pick up and save those who have "raised their frequencies," fall into the same category. These are but a few of the many "messages" being promiscuously broadcast today, purportedly from the space visitors. Such fallacies have no place in our associations with people of other worlds!

Contrary to such reports, the liaison teams from other planets are not here to rescue a selected few. They have come to help us develop a realistic, scientific and philosophical knowledge of the Cosmos, which can be readily absorbed by any Earthman who is really interested in brotherhood between men, with the purpose of establishing the age-old hope of peace on Earth, good will toward all. This relationship must be accomplished in our world before our planet can resume its rightful place in the system.

During the years that such false rumors and reports have been increasing in numbers, the thinking public has turned away, ofttimes in disgust, and has impatiently rejected the reality of interplanetary travelers, especially the validity of personal contacts of any sort, classifying them all as being in the same worthless category. Now, little by little, with scientific events developing as they are today, the thinkers are demanding logical explanations of that which can no longer be denied. But they want no fantasies or confidence games!

Right here let me say that I have no doubt that many people who receive "messages" of various types through the channels of trances, Ouija boards, automatic writing, etc., actually are convinced that their experiences are real and originate outside their own mind.

In reality, such experiences are produced by the subconscious and can be compared to dreams in which we see people, hear voices, hold intelligent conversations, and are often able to accomplish fantastic feats totally impossible to us during our waking hours.

The human mind is a complex, natural electronic machine, and the self-induced trance state is an open door to the subconscious. In these semi-hypnotic states, the subconscious initiates supposedly profound observations into the mysteries of philosophy, UFO's, world affairs and so on. When the receiver of these so-called messages awakens, he firmly believes that some outside agency was responsible for the information received. He fails to see the resemblance between the ordinary dream and the trance or mediumistic dream.

Many of the random thoughts that pass through the minds of people as they go about their daily chores would, if seized upon and carefully evaluated, yield valuable information direct from the universal storehouse of knowledge. These thoughts are, in essence, true telepathy, and useful in building the experience and knowledge required for true intellectual advancement. They do not come from spirits, either of this world or out of this world.

When a person has developed his ability to the point of correctly tuning in these thoughts of a universal nature, he will be channeled toward constructive rather than destructive purposes. Gone will be thoughts of divisions and personal aspirations. He will begin to see the answers behind age-old questions of an abstruse philosophical nature. He will become able to harness certain of Nature's forces, and the entire Cosmos will open and gradually reveal itself to him. Studies in this direction are truly of the sciences, regardless under what name one might wish to catalog them.

During the past quarter of a century, people in our world have been awakened and are more desirous than ever for better understanding. Some quickly see the shortcomings of psychic messages being given today, purportedly from the space travelers, and turn to seek elsewhere in their search for wisdom. Others are overcome with the pleasure granted the ego by false teachers, and stop to play for awhile. But, since eternity is just that, these children will in time tire of their play and again take up their search for true wisdom and understanding.

Telepathy is the inherent birthright of every human, but who knows the workings of his mind well enough to be capable of such communication, accurately received and understood? True, many in our world today are studying this science, but few have become masters of it—and I am not one of those few. The space people are experts in telepathy, both in sending and receiving. They know that it is characteristic of most Earthlings—even among close friends, and without intention of misunderstanding—to interpret what is heard according to what one expects to hear. When repeated, the information is given according to the hearer's interpretation, and is often totally different from the original meaning, thus creating frequent misunderstanding and confusion.

In addition, many Earthly languages have identical words with different meanings. Not only is this true within a single nation, but the same word is often interpreted entirely differently between nations. For instance, in the U.S.A. a radiogram is a wireless message. In Australia a radiogram is what we call a phonograph, or record player. There are many such differences, as one learns when traveling or studying more than one language.

Full understanding of the mind is important before one can become accurate in telepathy, for, to be a good receiver of thought, one must be able to completely eliminate personality.

The human mind is like a sponge that can be saturated with every impression that comes along. When it is habitually concerned with its own personal interests, it is impossible for it to receive a message accurately, regardless of its source. To do so requires total elimination of all personal interests. In other words, the line must be clear.

For instance, if two people are talking on a telephone, and one does all the talking, he is incapable of hearing what the other might be trying to tell him. The average Earthly mind is much like the incessant talker. It is seldom quiet enough to listen to anything or anyone. Even when it is in an apparent listening state it is forming questions to be asked later, or stopping to reason on what has been said, thus losing what is in the process of being said.

Again, one might compare most of those who are today claiming mental contact with the space people with a housewife who, having been away from home, returns to an empty and silent house. To have company, she turns on the radio or TV without selecting any particular program. She only wants the sound of someone's voice in the house to keep her company. The atmosphere around every planet, as well as space itself, is filled with thought forms, of both the past and present, and of every known characteristic.

Therefore he who, without understanding, opens his mind for "messages," makes himself the willing receiver for any passing thought regardless of its nature. That is why there are so many frightening messages and false promises being received. They are but repetitions of historic events through which mankind was brought into servitude of one kind or another, thereby losing its inherent birthright of peace, happiness and true freedom which can be assured only through wisdom, and respect between man and man.

The space travelers have recognized all these conditions. They do not condemn them, for they understand that they are one process of growing—unpleasant experiences. They know, too, that the material of which such experiences are composed will not stand up in the light of true understanding. It is for this reason that they have not used telepathy to convey information to the inhabitants of Earth.

Personal meetings are used along with *some* telepathy, as was my case, so that they can be reasonably sure the information they wish to convey is passed on correctly. Even so, there have been misunderstandings of their words, and inaccurate accounts given, through slight distortions by the receiver of the information. Telepathy by itself can never be relied on.

Another problem which the space travelers have met in their attempts to help their Earthly brothers is the matter of those who have endeavored to turn their coming into a religion. A number of cults have been established in their name of which they are in whole-hearted disapproval.

The interplanetarians are not superhuman; they are not gods, and do not want to be worshipped.

To them religion is the science of life to be lived as taught by Nature, with new thoughts and understanding constantly being given them by the Supreme Intelligence alone. They did not realize to what extent Earth people have been taught to accept religious interpretations handed down by others as gospel truth, with few ever daring to think for themselves on the subject.

Although the Brothers do not have religious rules and rituals as we on Earth, they do not condemn our practices. They know that all faiths are founded upon a pearl of wisdom. Divisions have been established solely by the ritualistic cloak worn. Basically all are the same.

Terrestrial man will never gain a working knowledge of Universal Law, or of his Creator, so long as he permits other men to do his thinking, accepting on faith alone interpretations of universal wisdom handed down through the centuries, along with errors in translations and personal selections of what was thought right for the people to know. He does not have to give up anything or alter religious beliefs to gain knowledge of the universe. All a man has to do is think for himself. He must merge his thinking with the whole creation instead of confining his thoughts to himself, or permitting others to censor his thoughts. Each must do his own work of rebuilding. As Emerson put it: "Gift is contrary to the law of the universe. . . . Serving others is serving . . ."

Understanding this, it is obvious why the interplanetary visitors do not want any cult or religion established in their name. Those organizing sects, or making a religion of the space people and their visitations, have been and are working right in line with the factions who would keep mankind in ignorance for the promotion of their own special benefits. Some leaders are innocently working in this respect. Others are working for self-aggrandizement. Some, I am sure, are being paid by the "Silence Group" whose greatest asset is keeping people from thinking for themselves, and thus in ignorance.

Whatever the purpose, all are spreading confusion in the path of sincere seekers. At the same time, ridicule is heaped upon the entire program by the man who dares to think for himself. He refuses to believe all that he is told by others until something reasonable enters the picture. Then he is able to build a conviction with a firm foundation.

Our interplanetary friends, who are as normal and human as you and I, could not allow such falseness, with its resultant confusion, to be built up and continued in regard to them and their visitations to Earth. They told me that it was most important that I should clear up the matter in the minds of Earthlings. It was to this end that the world tour was arranged. It is only in retrospect that I realize the foundation for such a program was started several years before.

It was set up from the very beginning by correspondence resulting from the publication of *Inside the Space Ships** in 1955, when certain individuals in nations throughout the world were enough impressed by the book to write to me.

---

*published as *Inside the Flying Saucers* by Paperback Library, Inc. (# 53-428, 60¢)

BOOK II

1. AMERICA TO NEW ZEALAND

In late 1956, my colleagues and I were spending a few months in Chapala, Jalisco, Mexico. Mail from all over the world continued to increase in volume. I realized that, after our vacation was over and we returned to the United States, something would have to be done to ease the workload on my secretary. It was on this vacation that I shot the 16-mm. color motion pictures of the huge domed spacecraft that hovered near the highway.

We returned to Palomar Terraces in early 1957. My secretary could not possibly cope with the increasing interest in the spacecraft.

My first book, co-authored with Desmond Leslie, and originally published in England, Canada, and the United States in 1953, had by this time been translated and published in at least a dozen other languages.

I had not been the first to alert people to the strange objects flying in the sky. Kenneth Arnold had reported unexplainable objects in 1947. Frank Scully, in his book *Behind the Flying Saucers*,* related the story of an unidentified craft that had crash-landed in New Mexico. The incident recorded in *Flying Saucers Have Landed* was the first account published in modern times of a personal meeting with a human being from another planet.

Desmond Leslie, a British subject of Irish ancestry, became interested in ancient accounts of strange aerial objects. As a result, he spent several years perusing old manuscripts and compiling data. His book was in the hands of a publisher in London when my personal meeting with a man from Venus was publicized in a western U.S.A. newspaper. This was world news and it soon reached England. Both the publisher and Desmond Leslie wrote to me for details of my contact.

I had received so many letters of inquiry about my ex-

*Henry Holt and Co., New York.

perience that I had my account of it put into manuscript form, with the intention of having it published in small booklets to send in answer to these letters. I sent this manuscript to Leslie's publisher. It was suggested that my experiences be added to his book to bring the account up to date. This was a great opportunity to fulfill the space people's request for me to present my information to the people.

After the book was published, I received a humorous letter from Leslie which said: "I don't know what has happened, George, but all the mediums have suddenly disposed of their Indian guides, etc., and have replaced them with space people traveling in Vimanas." This was all too true.

This trend toward mysticism was the beginning of the perversion of the real purpose for which the space people came to Earth. This distortion of truth has been perpetuated by opportunists and has caused world-wide confusion. This same distortion has hampered a scientific approach to the wonders of the universe. As I have stated before, the psychic groups have become excellent tools in the hands of the "Silence Group."

Bearing these conditions in mind, we realized that each sincere question should have a sincere answer; but how were we to accomplish such a great task?

In the course of one of my contacts I mentioned to the Brothers the problems I was having. They advised an excellent solution. Briefly it was this: I would write to correspondents from each country and ask them if they would be willing to receive all the mail from their own countries. In turn, they would receive a periodic letter from me which they could reproduce and pass on to all interested persons.

This was called our *Get Acquainted Program*. The coworkers' letters contained all the latest information from many countries, and the program worked splendidly to keep people informed. Cooperation was excellent and the program relieved much of the workload on my secretary and myself.

In 1958 I received a letter from Australia, saying that a group of people there would finance a trip to their country if I would consent to lecture for them. When groups in other countries heard of the Australian offer, they asked for a similar program.

The secretary of one group in Australia, Gordon L. Jamieson, wrote from Brisbane and explained that it would be impossible for me to take any money out of their country. All expenses such as plane fare, room and board, etc., would have to be taken care of by the respective groups. This proved to be true of all nations.

I was advised that it was of great importance that I accept this opportunity in order that the people of the world might be informed of the true purpose of the visitations from our space friends. It was agreed that I would start the tour in January, 1959.

Accordingly, on January 13th I left Los Angeles International Airport on the first leg of my world tour. Arrangements had been made for a two-day visit in Hawaii to break the long flight to New Zealand. This was a welcome event, for several correspondents and friends live in Hawaii and I wanted to meet them.

When the plane arrived my friends were there to meet me. In their customary "aloha" greeting, I was bedecked with leis; so many, in fact, that I could barely see over the top of them.

It was quite late that evening when my friends bade me goodnight. We had had an enjoyable visit and no one had noticed the clock. Before leaving, a request was made and granted to arrange an informal dinner party for the following evening where I could speak and answer questions of interested guests. It was thought that only a small group of thirty-five or so would attend. As it turned out, this number was more than doubled. Following a most enjoyable dinner, I gave a short lecture, after which the guests asked many questions. I was amazed by the eager response from people hungry for down-to-earth information about the spacecraft and their occupants. This held true throughout my entire tour, in every country which I had the pleasure of visiting.

During my two-day stay in Hawaii, I was taken by my kind hosts on a tour of the main island, Oahu. I took motion pictures up through Nuuanu Pali, a pass through the Koolau mountain range. This scenic route connects the eastern shore to the windward or western side of the island. From an observation point I could see the Bay View Memorial Park where victims of the Pearl Harbor attack are buried.

One of the unusual sights I noticed was the monkey-pod tree. The wood from these trees cannot be used for construction purposes, but, because of its unusual graining, it is widely used in making dishes, novelties and souvenirs.

On the way back from one day's lovely trip we passed through Tanyalas, a scenic drive through heavily wooded areas and beautiful homes. Night-blooming cereus covered the banks along the road. The view of Honolulu Harbor was an inspiring sight from the high points. The oriental architecture of the homes of wealthy Chinese and Japanese businessmen was very beautiful, seen through the magnificent trees and shrubbery lining the boulevards we traveled.

All too quickly time passed for me and I had to resume my trip. At the airport, before I boarded my plane for New Zealand, my friends extended hearty invitations for me to return to Hawaii when I could spend more time on the Islands. My short time there was so enjoyable that some day I'd like to return for an extended vacation.

Shortly after I boarded the plane in Honolulu, we were on our way to the next stop, the Fiji Islands. Here I had to change planes for one going to New Zealand. The one out of Honolulu was going straight to Australia. Upon arriving at Fiji, I found my plane was not scheduled to leave for over an hour, although it was standing on the runway. The outside temperature at this airport was 110 degrees. It didn't take long before we all looked like wet sponges, although the native workers didn't seem to notice the intense heat. The Qantas Airlines did their best for our comfort by providing cold drinks of all kinds to help quench our thirst.

We had no way of knowing how long the plane bound for New Zealand had been standing in the hot sun, but when the time arrived for us to go aboard, the heat inside was stifling. This did not last for long, however, for when we were airborne the plane cooled off so rapidly that we seemed to be freezing—and I had to put on my topcoat.

On Saturday, January 17th, we reached New Zealand and

landed at Whenuapai Airport in Auckland. Henk (sic) and Brenda Hinfelaar and UFO study group leaders from North Island were at the airport awaiting my arrival.

After clearing customs and freshening up a bit, we all had dinner and soon became good friends. These men and women had come to Auckland from all parts of North Island to meet me and plan my lecture schedules. The following Monday I was given a reception sponsored by the Auckland Group.

While in Auckland, I was called for a half-hour program on the local television station, at that time the only TV station in New Zealand. It was an interesting experience, as their equipment and methods of broadcasting differed greatly from those found in the United States.

The only problem I encountered in New Zealand was the tight schedule outlined for my tour. I had to request that one of the lectures be cancelled so that I could conserve my health and cover the remaining tour.

On January 20th, the first lecture took place in Kaikohe, a two-hour flight from Auckland. A small bus took us into town from Kaikohe's nearest airport, a distance of some twenty miles through rugged mountain terrain. Some of the passengers became ill from the wild ride and the driver had to stop for them. Later we could see the humorous side of the experience and decided that our driver should have been a flying saucer pilot.

That evening, a group meeting was held for the Kaihoke Saucer Club with the public lecture scheduled for the following evening. The club had reserved the largest hall available; nevertheless a lot of people were turned away for lack of seats.

Henk—who made this trip with me—and I had to be back in Auckland the next day, January 22nd, for a lecture in the Town Hall. Early in the morning on the 22nd, we gathered our belongings and left for the airport.

In Auckland the Town Hall seated 2,000 people, and the tickets had all been sold days in advance. Several hundred people were standing outside when we arrived at the hall. Inside, people were sitting in the stage wings and on the platform. For those who were unable to get inside, loudspeakers were connected to the public address system and placed outside so that they could at least hear what was being said.

The next morning I was called for an interview by the leading radio station of Auckland. All the radio stations in New Zealand are controlled by the government; other than that they are much the same as found in the United States. The television producers, radio stations and newspapers were all very considerate and helpful in New Zealand. A tape recording was made, which the government sent ahead of me to be played by radio the day before my arrival in each city. I did not encounter this courtesy outside of New Zealand.

It seems that the New Zealand government has a policy of cooperation in the fields of learning, much more than other nations; at least much more than the other nations I have visited. As a comparatively new cultural center, New Zealand seems to have a broad outlook toward the future and embraces all fields of endeavor.

I had entered the country on a visitor's visa, and it was necessary to obtain a written permit before I could lecture and show my films of spacecraft. The officials made out my permit for twelve months, an indication that the government in that dominion desires to have the truth presented to its people.

There were many requests for private lectures, which, unfortunately, I had to refuse. All but one scheduled lecture was completed during my six weeks in New Zealand.

I received an invitation asking me to visit the Maori king in the royal Mahinarangi House at Ngaruawahia. It turned out to be one of the most interesting experiences of my life.

The Maoris are a very intelligent and clever people. They have developed great artistic abilities and their buildings are covered with many varieties of designs, both symbolic and decorative.

Some of the people in our party were not known to the Maoris. According to their customs, this prevented us seeing the king, but he sent word through one of his chieftains that I was accepted by the Maoris and would be welcome at any time.

The official hostess, Sister Heeni, took us into the reception room or King's Audience Room as it is called. The room was very large and beautifully ornate. The wall-to-wall wool rug, with an all-over Maori design, was hand-woven. The cross-beams in the ceiling were hand-carved and colored and the rafters were painted with Maori symbols. The supporting pillars were covered with hand-woven matting of fine reeds, beautifully designed and colored. Large lounge chairs encircled the room.

As we went outside I noticed a great deal of Maori carving on all the other buildings. Along the front of the eaves and gateways are intricate red carvings depicting the figures that are displayed along the tops of pillars near the entrance. I was given permission to take pictures of the outsides of the buildings and the surrounding grounds.

While I was taking pictures of the entranceway, six white streaks of light flashed overhead. This caused much interest among the Maoris, as they were not vapor trails, and Sister Heeni said it was a good omen and very significant.

As we drove back to Hamilton, the spacecraft streaking through the sky seemed to follow us. This had happened on other occasions and I knew the Brothers felt that this was the time and place to make their presence known.

Some time later a Maori lady called on me, and we talked of many things relating to the space people. She mentioned that several of the Maori boys had been taken up for rides in spacecraft. In my next lecture I repeated her story.

On February 9, 1959, the *New Zealand Herald* printed a story to the effect that I had confused fact with a Maori legend concerning Rona, the Maori "Woman in the Moon." They were sure the story I had related about the Maori boys taking a ride was actually a repetition of the ancient Maori legend. This, of course, was not the case, but it does go to show how a speaker's words can be distorted.

The following Monday I was taken on a picnic and excursion to the Maori village of Whakarewarewa. Here in the thermal regions, hot water, the Pohutu Geyser, and bubbling mud come shooting up through the ground. Many of the hot-water pools are of different temperatures; some used for cooking, some for bathing and some for washing clothes. The warm water is so close to the surface that graves cannot be dug, and all bodies are placed in crypts above the ground.

The tremendous heat and steam are harnessed by the Geothermal Power Project of Wairokei and are used to heat many nearby communities. Natural steam roaring forth from wells drilled deep into the ground is an awesome sight. I took many feet of film in full color of the tremendous natural activity taking place in this area.

Time has a way of running out, and soon I had to leave this scenic wonderland and depart for my next lecture at Napier.

Shortly after reaching Napier, I was called by a newspaperman in regard to flying saucer sightings reported in a local newspaper. Although I had a good idea of what had been seen, I told him I would have to meet the people who reported seeing the spacecraft before I made any comment.

After talking to the reporter I picked up the local paper and read the article:

"FLYING SAUCERS REPORTED OVER LAKE TAUPO. (P.A.) Rotorua. Three Rotorua people say they watched not one, but dozens of flying saucers operating high above the township of Taupo in bright sunlight on Tuesday. The trio had just farewelled Mr. George Adamski, who claims to have contact with extra-terrestrial visitors, who was on his way to Napier.

"Mr. W. Miller, the local leader of the George Adamski Group, said that with his wife and Mr. N. West, he was sitting on the bank overlooking the lake at the end of Taupo's main street, at 3 P.M.

"Asked when they had seen the first flying saucer, the Millers who have been interested in flying saucers for two years, said: 'Yesterday.'

" 'We couldn't say how many there were, but we could have seen the same ones twice,' said Mr. Miller. Lying on their backs, they could not pick out verticle movement, nor estimate the height or size of the craft.

"In addition to these reported sightings, it is rumoured in Rotorua that many people, including more than 100 Maoris, saw two spacecraft flying in formation between Ngaruawahia and Hamilton last Sunday."

The spacecraft sightings seemed always to come at the right time to awaken public interest. This was one of the reasons we enjoyed overflow crowds at all the New Zealand lectures.

My lecture in Napier was scheduled for Wednesday, January 28th. I spent the few leisure hours before the lecture viewing the beautiful Napier scenery.

I strolled down a long park called The Marine Parade that extends through the city. One of the lovely features of the park was a magnificent bronze statue of the Maori maiden of the sea, "Pania of the Reef." Most of the places in New Zealand are named after Maori legendary figures, and mythological figures are depicted prominently in their buildings and statues.

According to legend, Pania fell in love with a Maori warrior and deserted the sea to live with him on land. Pania's people constantly pleaded with her to return home to the sea and forsake her love. She finally listened to her people and returned to her former home. A shoal or reef lying a few miles offshore has been named in her honor. The bronze statue of Pania is a beautiful portrait of feminine grace. She is seated on a rock with her right leg under the left. Her body is bare to the waist. A Maori flax skirt is artistically draped over her knees.

Another attraction in this beautiful park is the huge floral clock constructed by the citizens of Napier. Its face and numerals are of growing flowers in a variety of colors. I saw a number of similar clocks during my trip. All are very large and keep accurate time.

Next I toured the Kiwi Game Farm in Napier. The kiwi is the national bird of New Zealand. Nocturnal in its habits, this bird cannot fly, is about the size of a hen, and has a body covered with hair-like feathers. It has a long, curved beak and finds its food mostly by scent. I was allowed to enter the kiwi enclosure and took a few motion pictures. This was hard to do, as the kiwi always seeks dark corners, and was accomplished only through the kindness of the keeper, who took one of the birds out into the light. In its peculiar gait, it immediately returned to the darkness of its covered shed.

My public lecture in Napier was a huge success with standing room only in the large hall where it was held. Later a second lecture was given at the War Memorial in Napier Marine Gardens. This was to a group of some 100 researchers, and was also very successful.

My next lecture was scheduled for Sunday, February 1, in Wellington, the capitol of New Zealand. The lecture here was given in the Concert Chamber of Town Hall. This location lent prestige to the lecture. Thus, people who ordinarily would not have attended a flying saucer lecture in a less popular place found little hesitation in attending at Town Hall.

After the lecture in Wellington, I returned to Auckland and made plans for my next public lecture, scheduled for Wanganui. From Wanganui I journeyed to New Plymouth for a lecture on February 5th. The reception in New Plymouth was excellent. While I was waiting in my hotel lobby for a reporter, a French actress came over and wanted to know how I drew such large crowds to the lectures. I told her the interest lay not in me but in the subject I was presenting.

It is an established fact that a scientific approach to a controversial topic will draw more people. Intelligent people realize that the spacemen are in no way related to psychics and mysticism. This logical thinking on the part of the public has been the major factor responsible for the success of my books and lectures.

It was early twilight when the people began gathering in New Plymouth's hall on the evening of the lecture. A minister and members of his congregation had seen a large space ship cruise over the city. This caused much excitement and as I arrived, people were eagerly wondering if the space ship would return.

I explained to them that I had no control over such things, and for that matter, couldn't even arrange my own contacts. If I were selfishly disposed and could arrange contacts, I would be a millionaire. Many people have offered large sums of money to me and to others to arrange contacts for them. Naturally I have always refused such offers.

Bowing to public demand, I returned to Auckland for a

request lecture before leaving North Island for Christchurch in South Island.

Arriving in Christchurch by plane, I was met at the airport by nine South Island research group leaders. They were all splendid persons and proved to be gracious hosts. It was in this city I had the pleasure of meeting "Happi" Hill, a radio personality who is quite popular with the radio listeners. I had heard many favorable things about this man, and found him to be even finer than described. Hill acted as Master of Ceremonies for my lecture on February 10th. He gave a splendid introduction, and seemed to be keenly interested in the space people. Before I left Christchurch, he took motion pictures and made sound recordings of me, to be used later by the television and radio stations for their broadcasts.

In Timaru, my next stop, we had the assistance of a government man and the use of such equipment as a screen and projector, and an operator to run the film. I also made a tape recording to be broadcast on the local radio station after my departure from New Zealand.

Next I traveled south, down the coast to Dunedin, where my lecture was delivered in His Majesty's Theatre on Sunday, February 15th. This completed my tour of New Zealand, and I returned to Auckland to board a plane for Australia.

The success of my lecture tour in New Zealand was tremendous and the cooperation was excellent. New Zealand's population of two and one-half million people seemed open-minded and hungry for new adventures in life. If I were a young man, choosing a new land in which to live, I believe I would select New Zealand. The country offers many opportunities and the people are friendly and kind.

As in later chapters, I am unable to relate fully the scenic beauties of each nation I visited. I also am not able to introduce and do justice to the many friends whom I met along the way; friends who spared themselves no effort in considering my welfare. To do so, naming each individual and describing the warmth with which I was received in their homes and families, would enlarge this report into several volumes.

I sincerely hope that it will suffice for me to say that in every nation I visited during the tour, I found wonderful men and women who are dedicated to seeking out the peaceful, productive means by which we shall earn our rightful, dignified position among the civilizations of other planets. Their kindness and hospitality will never be forgotten.

2. AUSTRALIA

As MY PLANE came in for landing at Sidney, I felt an apprehension that seemed to foretell unpleasant events. I knew the opposition would not sit still when they learned that people were hungry for the truth, that hundreds were being turned away at each lecture.

As it happened, the Australian press was surprised by the response I had received in New Zealand, and the lectures were well-publicized by the majority of Australian newspapers. This, plus the fact that I had repeatedly exposed the fallacies of mysticism and psychic phenomena as far as the space ships and contacts were concerned, was a major challenge to the "Silence Group." They seemed determined to stop my lectures in Australia.

People who follow the flying saucer investigations are becoming aware of a curious pattern—or is it really so curious? Wherever I go, whenever I lecture, someone always tries—unsuccessfully—to disclaim my contacts or to link me with the mystic hucksters. Other contact claimants are as a rule seldom—if ever—attacked by the press. The major concentrated effort has been directed against me and my evidence.

Some flying saucer publications have published distorted or false reports of me, with no basis in fact. Many groups sit around Ouija boards or hold hands in a séance, and unwittingly serve the "Silence Group." These and similar thoughts passed through my mind as the plane taxied to a stop at the passenger ramp. I wondered how the opposition was going to deal with the problem I had thrust upon them. My questions were answered in a matter of hours.

I was met by Gordon Jamieson and Roy Russell from Brisbane, and directed through customs. As I left the customs office, a group of people converged upon me. They were space enthusiasts, UFO study group leaders, and reporters.

When introductions were completed, I learned a press conference had been arranged. The reporters asked many questions and later wrote articles concerning my visit to their country. Some of the reporters distorted my statements and wrote that I claimed to have visited Venus and Mars. Actually, I have never made such statements! When the press conference concluded, I inquired as to where I should stay. This was when I received the first indication that my own wishes were not considered.

My secretary had explicitly requested that I be accommodated in hotels and not in private homes. This request was completely ignored. I was given a choice of two accommodations: one with a doctor who lived far from the city; the other in an apartment building. I chose the apartment, and did not know at the time how far it was from the heart of the city. It turned out later that my only choice would have been the apartment.

My hostess was an astrologer. She was endeavoring to associate astrology with the space people and their craft. I explained to her that no connection existed between the two, but she refused to accept the logical facts. Like many people, she had closed her mind to any ideas which differed from her preconceived notions.

While arranging my lecture for the UFO group of Sydney, I learned the group did not want to sponsor me as an organization; still, they wished me to lecture for them. A foreigner in Australia must have a work permit. Lecturing is considered work, whether the lecturer is paid or not. This permit had not been issued, and since the group seemed reluctant to assist me in securing a permit, I became apprehensive. I was not sure that the government would allow me to lecture in Sydney.

During the pre-lecture press conference and radio-TV appearances, I could not mention the lecture because the situation was so uncertain. The time for the lecture was drawing near; tickets had been sold and many persons who wanted to attend could not be accommodated.

The committee in charge of the lecture arrangements continued to insist that a work permit was not necessary. At this point I grew weary, sensing that their actions might be part of a plan to stop the lecture tour by getting me into difficulty with the government. I refused to lecture without the permit. The whole situation seemed to be a plot, and later evidence confirmed my beliefs.

A committee member finally secured the work permit, and the group sponsored my lecture in Sydney. The lecture was very well received, and when it was over I was asked if I had a permit from the censor's office to show the film. This came as a surprise, because previous arrangements with the Immigration Department had supposedly taken care of the matter.

I replied that a permit had not been issued and stated that the film would not be shown again until official permission had been received in writing. The incident served to alert me that new efforts would be made to stop the lectures, or at least to prevent me from showing the film.

We finally went to the censor's office, set up a projector and showed the film. The officials seemed amazed at the films; and after the showing, a permit was issued. Now the trouble was ended, at least from that quarter! Once these problems had been solved and were out of the way, I found the people of Sydney to be very courteous and receptive.

On March 4th, I flew to Perth. There I met Bob Morrow who writes for the *South Western Times,* a large newspaper. Morrow was an interesting person and wrote many fine articles on space. I truly enjoyed my talks with him concerning the space people and their visits. My host in Perth, leader of the local flying saucer club, was a kind and hospitable person.

In Adelaide, after my second successful lecture in that city, a group of us were standing outside the hall waiting for transportation. One of the ladies sighted several space ships. Some of the ladies in the group observed the craft in detail before the ships passed out of sight.

A priest approached the group and asked me to lecture at the local orphanage. After the lecture a lovely luncheon was served by the sisters. All the children, priests, and sisters were very kind and seemed intensely interested in the space program.

As I was getting ready to leave for Melbourne, I was asked why the space ships did not land in Australia. I replied that they might after I had gone.

A landing did occur, much to their surprise! This landing took place before I left Adelaide, but was not publicized until I arrived in Melbourne. Imagine my surprise when I read in the *Sunday Mail* of March 28th, the following article:

"WE SAW A SPACE SHIP—Eerie Object Puzzles Town. By Staff Reporter John Pinkney. Did a space ship from an alien planet land this month in South Australia? Eerie happenings in the township of Purnong, 91 miles northeast of Adelaide, are prompting residents to ask this question seriously.

"In recent weeks weird, multi-colored objects have streaked across Purnong's skies—frightening the townsfolk. Two local men swear that on March 13th, they saw a huge dome-shaped craft take off from a field. The men are Mr. Percy Briggs, Purnong Landing carrier, and Mr. Carl Towill, postmaster at Claypans. Mr. Towill said: 'The thing was bigger than an airliner. Mr. Briggs and I are convinced that it was intelligently controlled.' The two men said they saw an enormous dome-shaped craft glowing in the dark and as they walked towards the mysterious object it rose silently into the air, hovered, then shot away at immense speed."

During my stay in Melbourne I enjoyed a warm welcome from the local UFO study group. I remained in their city from March 16th to 30th.

The press in both Adelaide and Melbourne was very cooperative. In Melbourne a photo was taken of me on top of a large building overlooking the city. A strong wind was blowing, and I have several times heard comments laughingly made that the picture made it look as though I was about to "take off." This photo and a number of my spacecraft pictures were combined with a lengthy feature article in *Today's Herald Newsreel* of March 19th.

The following Sunday night I appeared on *Meet The Press* program of Australia. The results of this appearance were most favorable. After the appearance I interrupted my visit in Melbourne to fly to Hobart, Tasmania for a private lecture.

Returning to Melbourne, I once again resumed my tour, going by plane to Brisbane where my stay proved to be more of a holiday than work. The good people of that city took care of my every need, and left me plenty of time for rest and relaxation.

As an introduction to one of my lectures in Brisbane, the students of a public school put on a show. The boys were made up with green grease paint, and were dressed as "green men from Mars." They wore little caps with antennae attached and presented a short drama. Then they encircled me and sang their version of a "Martian song and chant."

There was no rowdyism, nor were destructive tactics used. The Brisbane students were open-minded and eager to learn. The public listened attentively to the lecture.

Here, as elsewhere, hundreds were turned away and could not gain admission. I will always remember the fine cooperation of the press, the public, and the research group in Brisbane.

While there, I had an opportunity to see the Russian motion picture, *Blazing a Trail to the Stars*. Several scenes in the film were nearly identical with things I had seen inside the huge space ships. Some of these were things I had never mentioned to the public. Perhaps a Russian has been inside the spacecraft also? If the Russians continue to produce films as factual and interesting as that one, the American producers, with fantastic stories about "monsters from space," will be left far behind. In Europe I learned that American space films are considered gruesome. Most people overseas prefer the European films. They desire more factual presentations, and fewer of the "horrors from space."

Before leaving Brisbane I decided to take a brief tour through the Lone Pine Koala Sanctuary. This particular sanctuary was started in 1927 by Mr. Cam Reid and was the first privately owned and operated sanctuary in Australia.

The koala is a primitive type of animal. It carries its young similar to a kangaroo and subsists on leaves from the eucalyptus tree. It needs no water throughout its entire lifetime. The Lone Pine Sanctuary had 100 or more koalas who were tame and in perfect health, all having been bred at the sanctuary. A small zoo nearby housed other animals including the emu, kangaroo, wallaby, wallaroo, dingo, opossum and the python snake.

I found that the kangaroo is hunted and eaten in Australia, just as we do deer here in the United States. It is the main food for the Australian aborigine.

When I left the sanctuary I traveled fifteen miles down the Brisbane River by motor launch. It provided a very scenic and enjoyable river cruise all the way.

After my Australian lectures were completed, I flew to Darwin on the northern tip of Australia, to board the plane for London. The farewell party and the goodbyes at the Brisbane Airport will always be remembered. I was sorry that I could not continue an enjoyable stay with my new-found friends.

3. DARWIN TO ENGLAND

My PLANE left Darwin on the evening of April 16th, 1959. Ahead of me was a flight of about eleven thousand miles.

Our first refueling stop was at Singapore. Here it was very hot and humid. When I went into the airport lounge I found a telegram waiting for me, a request from the BBC in London, England, to appear on their program *Panorama* the following Monday. I accepted by wire, boarded the plane, and again was on my way.

Our next stop was Bangkok, capital of Thailand. Here three buses met our plane. The passengers were directed aboard the buses, and all were taken through the outskirts of the city to a club where we were served food and drinks. We dined on a terrace which gave an excellent view of this scenic city. It was very colorful; as in the States, people were coming and going all the time. I was interested in the natives and wondered what their reaction would be to the subject of space travel. Finally I found one who could speak English and engaged him in conversation. He gave me a new perspective on the matter.

118

There are records in some Far Eastern nations containing a great deal of information regarding earlier visits from the space people. These historical accounts tell of the ancient times when spacemen frequently visited Earth.

The man to whom I was talking said the people are not "holy" enough for spacecraft information. Only a few here and there could be given the information and they guarded it carefully until they felt the people could benefit from knowledge.

"That will probably not be for some time," I commented. "That depends upon the individual," he replied. "Some are awakening now, but the majority of the people are asleep."

And so it is. While it is not a question of how "holy" a person is, it is a question of how much understanding and knowledge the individual has gained. Some people are capable of opening their minds enough so that they can extend their thoughts and interests into space and wonder about our neighbors on other planets and their way of living. Others, those with closed minds, find themselves unable to think about anything beyond the confines of their own limited personal lives.

Our next stop was Calcutta, seventh largest city in the world, and the greatest center of industry in India. We landed at Dum Dum Airport where I was greeted by Dr. S. K. Maitra of Banaras Hindu University and a group of his friends and associates. Pictures were taken as I walked down the steps from the plane, and as I reached the ground a wreath of flowers was placed around my neck. A large number of natives standing outside the fence cheered and waved salutations as Dr. Maitra and his friends greeted me. I felt their heart-warming sincerity and appreciation of the message which I had been entrusted to give to the people of the world.

Dr. Maitra was dressed in a white linen cap, long white jacket and white trousers. His companions were all dressed in white also, but he alone wore the long white jacket. These garments were in contrast to the modernized industrial background of Calcutta.

I had corresponded with the good doctor for a number of years and knew that he and his friends wished to be brought up to date on the space people and their visits. I knew that Hindu history is filled with accounts of vehicles from space appearing on Earth, and of their occupants alerting Earthmen to the changes taking place on their planet. Dr. Maitra had many questions to ask regarding present-day conditions and the latest information from the Brothers.

Prior to my arrival, arrangements had been made through the University to permit me to visit with these friends, apart from the other tourists, so that we would not be interrupted. I was glad to answer many of their questions with information given by my friends from other planets. During our visit, I was asked to lecture to the students of the University; but, unfortunately, there was insufficient time, as my plane was due to leave. I felt badly about this and hope that some day I will be permitted to return and address the student body.

In India alone, through the efforts of Dr. Maitra and his friends, the significance of changing times has been recognized and an annual celebration has been observed on November 20th, in commemoration of my first meeting with a spaceman in 1952. In some publications of India, leading educators and men of science have contributed articles that substantiated earlier knowledge gained from Hindu history. They pleaded for greater friendship between Earth and our interplanetary visitors and a greater understanding among men of Earth.

I was sorry to leave these true friends, but too often one must depart from the pleasant and continue along the highway of life.

Our next stop was Karachi, bustling seaport capital of Pakistan, once known as "Kalachi," the land of sand dunes. One of the Karachi Airport officials, asking that his name be withheld, told me his people knew a great deal about space people and said that the population of his native territory had been aided in various ways by them.

"Some day, through the efforts of our neighbors from other planets," he said, "India and Pakistan will become as brothers in one big family. On one or two occasions in the past twelve years, some government officials and religious leaders have dined with the Visitors," he added.

I acted surprised. "What did they look like? You could be one, for they look no different from Earthmen," he replied. "Were you ever among the privileged ones?" I asked. "No," he said. "I received my information from a high government official who was present at the time." He indicated that more than one government of the world had had similar experiences.

"If these men would come out with what they know, it would probably help this troubled world immensely," I remarked. He replied that perhaps it would not help, and commented, "You see, in these days men are fighting over opinions, not truth, for they no longer know what the truth is."

Our conversation lasted for several minutes, during which he expressed the belief that some men will sacrifice family or whatever else is involved for self-gain.

Self-opinionated men, heads of the masses, are willing to sacrifice those they represent in order to prove their opinions and keep their positions. The world at present is being fed indigestible food by politicians and religious leaders, and is being made sick. That is why the men who know the truth cannot or will not speak. Any truth spoken now would be discredited by those two forces. The public has been schooled to accept official opinions as facts.

I was interested in hearing this analysis of world conditions expressed by an official in the airport of a Far Eastern nation. It was in total agreement with what I had learned in my travels, as well as with what I had been told by the Brothers. Much as I would have liked to have continued my visit with this interesting person, plane time had arrived and I had to go aboard and continue on once again.

When we left Darwin, we had been told that no photographs could be taken while we were in flight. This was disappointing; for, as we flew over Egypt, I missed a chance for some beautiful shots of the pyramids. I also saw the reasons for the restrictions, for there were many military planes on the ground and ready for action. These were plainly visible as we flew over Cairo.

After a brief stop in Cairo we went on to Athens. I had to forego the pleasure of seeing the Parthenon, the Temple of Nike, the Acropolis and other famed sights, due to lack of time. We stopped briefly in Rome, then proceeded on to England. I arrived in London on April 18th, 1959.

The flight into London was very beautiful. Desmond Leslie and Mr. John M. Lade met me at the airport and took me to the Hyde Park Hotel, where reservations had been made before my arrival.

I had dinner with Desmond Leslie, then appeared on the BBC program *In Town Tonight*. The next day was Sunday, so I spent it with Desmond Leslie and his family, who showed me the sights around London.

Monday I was scheduled to appear on the BBC television program *Panorama*. According to reports I had received, this program is one of their best TV shows, with an estimated viewing audience of nine million. My appearance was to be in the form of a debate with Patrick Moore, well-known British astronomer.

We arrived at the studio early and were having lunch when Mr. Moore came in. I was introduced to him and we chatted a moment before the program director called him to the opposite side of the room. It appeared that the director was coaching him in regards to how the program should be handled. I was unconcerned, for as I shook his hand I had realized that man to man we were friends; but he had a job to do, and as a recognized authority of astronomy he would have to oppose me and try to prove me false. He had a daily program on the BBC network and at least a portion of his income depended on that program.

As the show started, he tried to disqualify my knowledge of astronomy, but his attempts were unsuccessful. The program was entirely too short, and, unfortunately, public opinion went against him. Even the most hardened critic stated in the next day's press that I had won the debate by "sheer dignity." Public reaction was very great and Moore was given two months' leave of absence from the show.

I regretted this turn of events for him. At the same time, I realized that if it had not been for the assistance from my space friends Moore could have massacred me before the public. It took more than terrestrial knowledge to see through the methods which were used in his attempt to discredit me. If I had not been advised by the space people during my trip, I would have easily succumbed.

As a man and a scientist, I have the utmost respect for Patrick Moore. After the show was over we went to my hotel. Desmond Leslie and several other people accompanied us. There we had an interesting pro-and-con discussion about the program.

It seemed to me that Moore was satisfied with the results of the debate. As I think it over now, he may have wanted it to turn out that way, for he had been one of the British astronomers, along with Dr. H. Percy Wilkins, who had confirmed the existence of the Mare Crisium bridge on the moon. He must have known for certain that someone had been using the moon as a base of operations, and the only logical ones were people from other planets.

A public lecture had been scheduled for Tuesday, April 21st, at Tunbridge Wells. When we arrived by car, I was cordially received by Air Chief Marshal Lord Dowding. I asked if the lecture and film permits had been obtained and was told that an official had said they would not be necessary. Lord Dowding assured me this was correct, but I knew better.

Upon my arrival in the country my passport had been stamped "Tourist." That meant I was not to work in England, paid or not. This presented a big problem for I refused to work without the written permit. All tickets had been sold, and Lord Dowding was very perturbed. He called his attorney, who told him it was quite all right to proceed with the lecture. Another friend talked with the attorney and was told the same. Then I was asked to speak with the attorney. When he said everything was in order, I asked him if he would put that in writing. When he said, "No, it is not necessary," I stood my ground.

By this time they all thought I was pretty stubborn and didn't know the law. I was sorry to put them to so much bother, but I did not dare give the opposition a legal loophole by which they might stop my lectures or confiscate my film.

The people in England were sincere, but were not aware of what was involved. They had not been alerted to the powerful influence of the "Silence Group," and to the lengths to which this group had gone to keep the truth from the public.

It was finally decided that Lord Dowding would preside and I would act as guest speaker to answer people's questions. This would be satisfactory, since it was handled as a club meeting and no permit was necessary.

I was seated on the platform with Lord Dowding. He explained to the audience that, due to certain circumstances, the lecture as scheduled would not be given, but that I would answer questions pertaining to my experiences. He also announced that if any wished their money refunded, it would be done. No one asked for a refund. Lord Dowding asked the first question and the meeting lasted two hours.

When we returned to London, a written permit was obtained from the Ministry of Labour and National Service. This permit was good for the whole of the British Isles.

My next lecture was scheduled for April 23rd at Weston-super-Mare. Desmond Leslie drove me to the railroad station and helped me get settled in my compartment. When we entered the compartment reserved for me, we were surprised to find another passenger seated there. The train was ready to move so Desmond didn't have a chance to inform him of his mistake.

Desmond and I shook hands and said goodbye just as the train started to move. After a short interval, the man in my compartment started a conversation. To my amazement, he was a spaceman working as a scientist on projects for the British government! He, and countless others like him, are working in various scientific projects for every government in the world. In this way the space people can help us reach out into space, with our own science and our own ships, bringing us nearer to the understanding that abundant intelligent life exists throughout the Cosmos. This is the only way the people of Earth can be awakened from their state of lethargy and apathy, into the realization that a far greater destiny than they ever imagined awaits them.

Weston-super-Mare was a very pretty coastal town, situated where Bristol Channel and the River Severn blend. The hall chosen for the lecture was filled to capacity with people from all over the western coastal area. A great deal of interest was displayed toward the lecture and the films, and many intelligent questions were asked.

During my stay in Bournemouth, friends arranged a meeting for me with Leonard G. Cramp, author of *Space, Gravity and the Flying Saucer*.* Cramp, a member of the Interplanetary Society of England and an expert engineer, proved the authenticity of my still photographs by comparing them with Stephen Darbishire's photos of the famous "Coniston Saucer." The comparison, by means of orthographic projection, proved the space ship photographed in England had the same ratio of dimensions as the spacecraft I photographed hovering over Palomar Gardens in Southern California.

Cramp also proved that it would be impossible for someone to copy my photographs and make a model of a space ship that would have exactly the same ratios of dimension when photographed from a different angle. The scales of measurement, from porthole to flange, cabin height and diameter, and top to bottom, were all identical in both the English and American photographs!

After the Bournemouth lecture, I returned to London and stayed with Desmond Leslie and his family. Another lecture was held in Caxton Hall on April 28th.

The next lecture was held at the Birmingham Institute on April 29th. All arrangements for the lecture had been placed in the hands of the Institute faculty. This well-known body, dedicated to scientific truth and culture, offers its services to persons whom it determines are worthy of merit. The Institute Hall, with a seating capacity of more than 750, was filled to overflowing. The audience gave serious attention.

Manchester was next on my schedule. Here, on May 1st, 1959, I gave a lecture in Houldsworth Hall. Success here was equal to that of all previous efforts. In each place my film was very well received and heartily applauded.

Throughout the British Isles there were many more lectures than those specifically mentioned here. In Scotland,

*British Book Centre, Inc., New York.

where the weather was cold with snow and penetrating winds, I contracted a sore throat and a cold. These became so severe than on May 4th I telegraphed a message to Desmond Leslie: "No more lectures until I get over my cold."

The brief rest which followed gave me a chance to partly regain my health, so that I could go on to one of the most heart-warming experiences of my lecture tour: a private audience with Her Majesty Queen Juliana of the Netherlands.

4. THE ROYAL AUDIENCE

DURING MY STAY in Brisbane I received a letter from Rey d'Aquila of The Hague, Netherlands, requesting me to attend an interview with Queen Juliana on May 18th, 1959. The letter requested an immediate reply. I sent a cable confirming receipt of the letter and consenting to the interview.

Toward the end of April, when I returned to London from lectures in outlying cities of the British Isles, the rumor was out that I was to have an interview with Queen Juliana. I was at the home of Desmond Leslie when the telephone rang. It was a reporter asking for verification of the interview. I admitted only that such a rumor existed, and did not confirm anything.

The reporter was cautioned not to publish anything until it had been confirmed. He agreed to await confirmation, out of respect for Queen Juliana, but his respect was apparently short-lived.

The *Daily Herald* of April 29th, 1959, London, published the following article under the heading, "Juliana's New Joy—Flying Saucers." The reporter gave this account: "I checked with Juliana's secretary. 'Yes,' the secretary said over the phone from Holland. 'Her Majesty has asked Mr. Adamski to confidential talks. More than that I cannot disclose. The talk will be between the two of them alone.'"

The newspaper accounts which claimed I told reporters of the forthcoming meeting with Queen Juliana were entirely false. One thing is certain: the press was furious. The reporters could not get any information from me so they fabricated stories to save face (and perhaps to protect their jobs!). Newspapers all over the United States copied these false reports and added comments as they passed them on.

An article in the Los Angeles *Examiner* of May 19th, entitled "In Dutch On Saucer Discussion," stated: "The press has given Adamski, from Los Angeles, a chilly reception. The Catholic People's Party newspaper *De Volkskrant*, said, for example: 'We are not opposed to a court jester on the green lawns of the Royal Palace, provided he is not taken for an astronomical philosopher.' "

Soon after the newspaper *De Volkskrant* criticized my interview with Queen Juliana, several other Dutch papers followed suit and began to speak in a critical vein. The more dignified papers, however, presented straightforward accounts like the following:

"QUEEN JULIANA SEES U.S. WRITER, Hour's Discussion on Space Travel, from our correspondent, THE HAGUE, May 19. Queen Juliana and the Prince of the Netherlands today received, at Soestdijk Palace, Mr. George Adamski, the American author of several books on space travel. The Queen and Prince Bernhard had a talk lasting about an hour with Mr. Adamski. It is understood that the talk was of a purely informative character. The Queen and Prince Bernhard wanted to become acquainted with Mr. Adamski and his views.

"Those who were present at the conversation included Mr. C. Kolff, president of the Royal Netherlands Society for Aviation, Lieuetenant-General H. Schaper, Chief of the Royal Netherlands Air Staff, Professor Jongbloed, of Utrecht University, an expert in medical science dealing with aviation, and Professor Rooy, of Amsterdam University, who gives lectures on mass communication.

"Mr. Adamski, who claims to have flown round the moon in a flying saucer and to have been in contact with inhabitants of the planet Venus, is lecturing in The Hague and Amsterdam."

As I am a common man with no title or position, some newspapers questioned the Queen's right to invite me to the palace. A true ruler, or representative of the people, can gain knowledge from the lowest as well as the highest sources.

The press called the Queen gullible and accused her of falling for strange things. This is not true. She is only interested in all new things of life, as a ruler should be. We are living in times when on every hand things are changing. Unless the rulers are well informed, they cannot serve their people well.

Queen Juliana has the welfare of her people at heart. Therefore she has an open mind that permits her to look at all facets of life, not bowing to the dictates of the few; and so she was not persuaded to cancel the appointment.

At this time I will relate the true facts of my interview with the Queen. They have never been published before. The press reports quoting alleged questions and answers from the interview were falsified, as no reporters were allowed inside the palace during the interview!

I left London and arrived in Amsterdam on the 15th of May, 1959. Miss Rey d'Aquila and some newspaper reporters were at the airport to meet me. I was still suffering from the cold I had caught in Scotland, so I excused myself and was taken to a small hotel on the outskirts of Amsterdam.

The next afternoon I was called to a television rehearsal for a program that was to be given that evening. This was on May 16th, and I showed my film on the program. The reception by the public of my subject and the film was very good.

After the rehearsal, we drove back to the hotel, picked up my luggage and left for The Hague. Miss d'Aquila had arranged transportation by automobile, and I arrived at The Hague about midnight.

My hotel was in a quiet residential district, across the street from a beautiful park. The first day was set aside for me to rest. That morning I unpacked my camera and walked through the park to the ocean. Several restful hours were spent strolling around and photographing the local scenery.

I had been placed in this secluded hotel purposely to avoid the press. When newsmen could not locate me, they became very irritated. Those in charge of publicity would not say where I was staying, and the manager of the hotel had been given orders not to reveal my presence. For one day and evening I was able to relax.

On the morning of May 18th, I had breakfast and readied myself for the visit to Soestdijk Palace near Utrecht. The palace car was to call for me at 10:30 A.M. This was an informal meeting, so my business suit was proper attire. I had been carefully coached on the proper etiquette and conduct in the presence of my royal hosts. When the car arrived, I was introduced to the chauffeur who held the door open as I entered. To evade the press, we avoided the customary highway to the palace.

We entered the palace garden through a gate opened by a guard who saluted smartly as we passed. I noticed the highway in front of the palace was empty as we turned into the grounds. A winding driveway, bordered by massive shrubs, brought us to the huge entrance. My mind was so taken up in trying to remember all the instructions I had been given that I failed to notice much about the palace itself, except that it was white. The chauffeur had spoken very few words as we rode along and had given me a mint to relieve my throat when I coughed.

It was 11:00 A.M. when the car stopped in front of the entrance. A uniformed attendant opened the door, saluted, and escorted me up the broad steps to the palace doors, which were opened by two doormen dressed in royal blue, who also saluted. When I entered, one of these men helped me our of my top coat and muffler; the other escorted me into a large library with a high ceiling.

I had been nervous with anticipation, but a feeling of calm and ease came over me as I stood in the presence of the Queen. She and the others present were standing when I entered the room. The Queen's secretary came forward and introduced me to Her Majesty, Queen Juliana. In turn, I was presented to Prince Bernhard; Lt. General Schaper, Chief of the Royal Netherlands Air Staff; Professor Jongbloed, of Aerial Medicine; Dr. M. Rooy, Telecommunications; and Mr. Kolff, President of the Royal Netherlands Society for Aviation.

When the Queen acknowledged the introduction, I completely forgot all the instructions and could not remember the formalities that should have been followed. Instead, I acted upon my feelings and was at ease, for here was a feeling of welcome as among friends.

The Queen graciously asked if I drank coffee. When I replied that I did, coffee was served in large cups of beautiful design, while we remained standing. After all had been served, we were asked to be seated. That coffee was the best I had had since leaving America!

We were at one end of the library, seated in lounge chairs assembled in a horseshoe position. Directly across from me sat the Queen. Next to her was the Prince, and on my right, next to the Prince, was a gentleman who acted as spokesman for him. As I remember, this gentleman was Mr. Kolff. Seated on my left were the other three gentlemen already named. The secretary was seated a little apart from the others.

Small pastries were served, and as we sat enjoying the refreshments and indulging in informal conversation, I noted that Her Majesty wore a light blue frock. The men were dressed in black suits with white shirts and black ties.

Cigarettes were passed. Then the secretary opened the topic for which I had been summoned. She referred to my two books and asked a question regarding my trip around the moon. I was aware of having been granted only forty-five minutes, so I made my answers as brief as possible.

The astronomer and Air Force chief asked questions next, trying to discredit the interplanetary visitors. As I think of it now, perhaps my answer was a little rude in the presence of royalty, for I said: "I have known of no major officials of our Air Force, and few astronomers, who have told what they actually know about the visitors from space. It is a known fact that the secret files and confidential reports of the Air Force have never been released to the public, or even to high officers in the government. I am inclined to believe this applies to all governments." I think Her Majesty knew exactly what I meant, for she gave a tiny smile of acknowledgment.

I pointed out that most of the findings of our Earth satellite had been published in my books at least three years before.

Many questions were asked about inhabitants of other

planets. I retold much of what I had written in my second book. The major questions of our conference dealt with our future in outer space.

Awareness of time was lost as we all grew interested in the conversation about outer space. What began as a forty-five-minute interview lasted two hours. Finally the Queen reminded me that my lecture started in less than an hour. Interest was so great in the topic that, if it had not been for the lecture, we could have kept talking for hours.

When the Queen reminded me of the time, I arose and we all shook hands in a very friendly manner. I was deeply impressed with the firm sincere grasp of Her Majesty and the Prince. The spokesman for the Prince escorted me to the car. During the conference he had stated he would like to take a trip with the space people and he repeated the request as we descended the steps to the waiting car.

As we were leaving the Palace grounds, I noticed a large group of people standing across the highway and facing the Palace. As the car came through the gate, many of these people gave the familiar salute. Possibly they only wanted to get a look at the common man who had been granted a private interview with the Queen, and whom the press had described as an "objectionable" visitor. On the fast trip back to the hotel, I noticed crowds of people along the highways, saluting as we passed.

Arriving at the hotel, we found a car waiting to take me to the lecture at The Hague. The Queen's chauffeur asked if he might attend the lecture and was granted permission to do so.

Due to the long interview at the Palace, I arrived twenty minutes late at the lecture hall where a capacity crowd was waiting. The people present were filled with curiosity and anticipation in regard to my meeting with Queen Juliana. Reporters especially were insistent that I give them all the details. This I could not do, for the meeting had been on a level of dignity that denied me the privilege of speaking until the Queen spoke first. All I could say was: "The Queen was very kind, and if there were more people like her the world would be a better place to live in." A tremendous burst of applause took place, and from there on the lecture proceeded as normal.

After the lecture, the reporters crowded around me asking,

"What did the Queen say?" "It is the Queen's honor to speak first," I replied. This made the press very dissatisfied with me. Some went so far as to write up a fictitious interview, complete with questions and answers.

When I returned to my hotel I was grateful that no one knew where I was, for now I could relax and go over the events of the day.

A radio was in my room, and the next morning I tuned it to the BBC since I could not understand the Dutch of local stations. On an early-morning program called *The News of Europe,* I was very much surprised to hear a report from a Russian scientist stating that the moon was not composed of volcanic dust, but rather of granite formations similar to Earth. Many green spots that looked like vegetation had been observed on the other side of the moon. This confirmed some of the things I had told the Queen during our two-hour conference.

I was curious to know just how the Russians had gained this information. My friends and I discussed the possibilities later that morning. Was it possible that a Russian had made a trip as I had, or did they receive the information from their moon shot that went into orbit around the sun? (Information received at the time of this writing seems to confirm that they did.)

Before the morning was over I was asked if I would accept an interview with Fox Movietone in downtown Hague. I would be called for and taken to the appointed place so I agreed.

The selected place was a large hotel in the center of town. Our car was parked across the street from the building. I was told to walk across the street and enter the hotel. Cameras were ready and set for operation, but I had to rehearse the walk several times before pictures were finally taken. In the final take, the large glass doors, framed in brass, opened automatically and I entered the hotel.

I was greeted by many people, including the manager of the hotel, and received the customary salute. This was not photographed. I was taken to a large room where cameras and sound equipment were in place. Here I was seated beside a small mahogany table which held a bouquet of American

Beauty roses. My interrogator was seated on my right. His first question was: "The world wants to know what the Queen had to say."

My answer was that Her Majesty and His Royal Highness were deeply interested in the future of outer space developments. The interrogator was very dissatisfied with my reply and tried to get me to relate our conversation in some detail. When I refused, he hurried through the other questions, and the news conference was over. I was told this newsreel would be shown all over the world, but I have no reports of it ever having been shown.

It is interesting to note that, after my visit to the Palace, wherever I went in Holland I received the salute from those who recognized me. Perhaps this is a customary honor paid to one who has been received by the Queen.

On Friday May 22nd, I received an invitation from the manager of the City Theatre in downtown Amsterdam, to attend the preview of an Italian film, *Death Comes From Outer Space*.

The death that came from outer space was a gigantic asteroid traveling at terrific speed directly toward the earth. This asteroid was formed from all the debris blown into space by our atomic and hydrogen bomb explosions. The people of Earth were in a panic, for they were warned that at any moment it could hit our planet and cause complete destruction. Meanwhile, huge tidal waves and heavy earthquakes were wreaking havoc in many places throughout the world.

The scientists of all nations called upon the military in every other nation to aim their atomic missiles at the asteroid and to fire simultaneously. In this way the asteroid was destroyed by the same weapons that had caused its creation.

Representatives of the press were present at the showing. After it was over, I was asked if such things could happen in real life. I replied that it could and gave the following explanation:

"The lightning bolt is created from invisible particles of matter that are fused together by the terrific heat of a natural electrical discharge. It is entirely possible for the millions of tons of debris that have been blown into the upper regions of the earth's atmosphere to come together and form an artificial asteroid. The larger the mass of debris, the more attraction it would have for additional particles."

This picture alerted me to the possibility that radiation and fallout are not the only dangers we might be facing from our atomic explosions.

Reports have come from Mexico stating that a huge fireball crashed into a mountain just before the disastrous earthquake there in August of 1959.

Recently several planes have reportedly hit objects from space. Some have survived; others have crashed to their doom. Could they have crashed into some of the high-energy pockets left by our explosions?

Some of these man-made asteroids burn and glow, and could be mistaken for ordinary meteorites. This may also be the answer to some of the fireballs that have been reported.

By way of closing this chapter, I would like to reproduce in part a letter concerning the lecture in Amsterdam, sent to co-workers in The Netherlands area. It was written by Miss Rey d'Aquila, dated June 13th, 1959, and reads as follows:

"At the end of the lecture in Amsterdam, Professor E. L. Seelliger of Bergan (NH), physicist and former Delft Professor, stepped on the platform and thanked 'our friend Adamski' in public for the things that he had brought us. Quoting him exactly: 'The things that we have heard may sound strange to most of us, if not to all, but strange things happen every day, if our eyes are open. I hope that we will be open-minded and benefit from the things we have heard today.'

"The audience applauded heartily. (Inside information: Professor Seelliger is in good relation to the Queen and if we take his mental courage and her interest and deep understanding, we may conclude that after all George Adamaski's visit to our country has been a successful one and the stepping stone to a better future.)"

Regarding my interview with the Queen, I will again quote from the report: "But one thing we can say for sure, no press reporters were present. So what the press had further to say about his audience was a big lie from the first to the last line! *Paris Match*, for instance, carried a wholly imaginative 'Interview With The Queen', complete with questions and answers!"

I wish those imaginative reporters could have been present

during my interview with Queen Juliana. They might have learned something of dignity, kindness and gentility, from a great woman who rules her country with wisdom and love.

5. THE ZURICH INCIDENT

MY TRAIN arrived in Basel, Switzerland from Holland on Saturday evening, May 23rd. Mrs. Lou Zinsstag, a Swiss researcher, and some of her friends met me at the station.

These fine friendly people introduced themselves. Then we proceeded to a lovely hotel on the Rhine River. Centrally located, this hotel afforded a beautiful view of the river and surrounding country.

The next day, Sunday, I had a restful visit at the home of Mrs. Zinsstag. Monday morning we held a special preview of the film for the Basel police and local press. Tuesday we drove to a small hotel on the outskirts of Zurich.

The critical accounts published in Holland were being reprinted by the Swiss press, and my friends desired to protect me as much as possible. I appreciated their thoughtfulness, for I was tired and feeling below par. Swiss reporters bombarded me with the same questions that had been asked in Holland. My answers likewise were the same: it was the Queen's honor to speak first.

My first lecture in Zurich, May 26, was most successful. Unfortunately, many people had to be turned away because of lack of seating capacity. When the lecture was over and many had left the hall, a small group of about twenty-five persons remained to ask questions.

One man accused Mrs. Zinsstag of submitting a special list of questions instead of the ones asked by the audience. He also accused me of impersonating the real George Adamski! We later learned the man had been placed in the audience to start trouble, but apparently he lost his nerve in front of so many people.

This was our first warning of organized resistance, but despite this incident we proceeded to the second lecture in Zurich.

The Chief of Police in Zurich called and asked for a private showing of my film. This seemed a strange request as I had already shown the film at the first lecture. However, I agreed to meet with him at the appointed time.

As before, I requested a written permit to lecture and show the film. I already had the permits for Zurich, and I wondered why the private showing had been requested. I believe the real reason was that the indisputable evidence in the film was beginning to disturb the "Silence Group."

The meeting with the Chief of Police was pleasant. At the conclusion of the film he remarked that it was very surprising and that he had enjoyed seeing it. I think he was amazed to see that the film showed a large metallic space ship, and not just vague lights in the sky.

While we were driving him from the showing to his office, he chatted about traffic problems in his city, and inquired about similar problems in California. As he left the car, he said he would be at the next lecture with some of his officers, adding the comment that this is customary at all public gatherings.

On the morning of the second Zurich lecture, Mrs. Zinsstag and I had a very pleasant interview with two reporters of the German weekly news magazine *Der Spiegel*. The reporters asked many questions in perfect English.

Despite all of the previous skeptical publicity, *Der Spiegel* published a long extract of our interview, correctly translated. They did leave out some rather important links, and thus imparted an ever so slight "leg pulling" slant to it. The interview had lasted more than two hours though, and it would have been impossible to print all that had been said. Considering everything, the magazine displayed a high amount of courage and independence.

The Zurich police attended the next lecture, on the evening of May 29th. The puzzling thing was, they were all in civilian clothes instead of in uniform. According to a report later published by Mrs. Zinsstag:

"Three hundred students were seated strategically among 700 listeners. The reception of George Adamski by this majority was very warm and friendly. The start was good, but from the first, the students carried through their disturbance plan in a carefully studied crescendo. First clapping, stamping after

136

every sentence, then hollering, singing . . . After some time a nice man from the public asked for peace, but to no avail. The storm grew worse and worse, they started throwing things around, first into the public, then at us on the platform. Already before nine o'clock the organizers had called for the police, but no police showed up. Only when another listener came up and asked after the police a plain-clothes man came up slowly and said: 'Oh, we have been here for some time!' He then spoke in a rather weak voice and with still weaker arguments to the students and to the public; some people had started fighting with the students. His speech failed, of course; in the general uproar one was not even aware that he was from the police! Only those seated next to the platform had grasped the fact. How could anyone expect plain-clothes men to restore order in such a tohuwabchu [Sic]! There was something very fishy about those uniformless policemen.

"The students now started throwing fruit around. We decided to go on and show the film. Before the hall was darkened I explained its content in the way I had learned, and it was comparatively quiet in the hall until it got dark. The the culmination point came. The rowdies used children's trumpets and other noisy instruments and also fireworks and firecrackers.

"How well everything had been prepared. This shows from the fact that from the very beginning they shot powerful searchlights on the screen so that the pictures were barely visible. These strong lights were no ordinary torches, but must have been attached to the electrical wiring system of the hall. After we had gotten half way through the film, a beer bottle was thrown from the gallery toward the platform, hitting a lady on the shoulder. Some people cried out, and then the police ordered, 'Lights at once.' This was the end of the show.

"The most important paper of Switzerland, the *Neue Zuercher Zeitung,* wrote a completely false report the next day, stating that the one thing which had functioned on this evening had been the Zurich police! Since we made a tape, we are in possession of the policeman's speech . . . we can easily disprove this statement in a future publication . . . Needless to say that the big majority of the newspapers followed the story of their big brother, the most important financial and commercial paper in this country and the whole German-speaking part of Europe."

I was taken from the hall via the back door, through several buildings, to a small café on another street. Several students followed. One young chap who spoke English was admitted to the café. He acted as the spokesman for the rest of the group.

"I'm here to offer an apology to you," he began. "There were a few of us who tried to listen to what you said. We heard the nice things you said about Dr. Zwicky, the scientist. We had been told you would try to discredit Dr. Zwicky and modern astronomy. This was a demonstration in protest and in defense of both."

The next day reports started coming to us. We were told that the men of the Eidgenoessische Technische Hochschule University were the organizers of the disturbance at my lecture. However, they had no doubt received their instructions from higher up.

As I reviewed the events of the night before, the picture became increasingly clear. The private viewing of my film by the police chief, the lack of cooperation from the police at my lecture, and the powerful lights thrown on the screen to prevent the public from seeing the rest of my pictures, all added up to one thing.

The overwhelming onslaught of truth apparently had the "Silence Group" greatly worried. They had tried to make a last stand, hoping to succeed where they had failed before.

I realized then that the evidence most likely to cause them to go further in their efforts to stop me was my motion picture film of spacecraft. As I stated toward the beginning of this book, I had had my first trouble with the film in Sydney, Australia. I had also learned that some of the police were working with the "Silence Group." Many newspapers had been given orders on what to print. Each time these papers carried an article about my lectures, they would also attack my films.

During a lecture tour into the Pacific Northwest, U.S.A., prior to my leaving on this world trip, one of the largest newspapers in Seattle, Washington, had stated to my colleague, C. A. Honey, that they had been given orders not to print complimentary material about UFO's. They tried to refuse taking a regular paid advertisement for my Seattle lecture. Mr. Honey finally talked the advertising department into taking it, after stating that it was a shame that newspaper men were not as bold and impartial today as they were in years gone by! In the days before we had a controlled press, fearless editors would have screamed to high heaven if someone had threatened them and forbidden them to print certain types of information. More than one newspaper editor had admitted having orders he dared not violate, in regard to publicizing the spacecraft and their occupants.

In their attempt to discredit me, the Swiss instigators revealed the lack of neutrality in their country. The good people of Switzerland suffered the embarrassment.

An American physicist just happened to lecture in Basel the same night as my lecture in Zurich. He tipped his hand as to whom he was working for when he made the statement, according to the press, that he would answer any questions on flying saucers, provided the question was accompanied by one hundred Swiss francs. The money was to be given to a charitable institution. Needless to say, no questions were asked.

When I returned to Basel, a reporter for one of the large papers of Zurich asked if I would accept an apology for what had happened. I had been told previously that the police and the organizers of the demonstration were in trouble, and had been severely criticized by one of the papers.

My own feeling was that this reporter had been sent by the officials of Zurich to try and modify the repercussions of what had taken place. My reply to him was the same that I had given to the students. The apology should be given to the Swiss people and not to me, for the incident had placed them in a bad light all over the world.

The rapid pace of my lecture tour soon began to have its effect on me. Mrs. Zinsstag became concerned with my extreme fatigue and persistent cough, and insisted that I see a doctor.

A complete physical examination showed a congestion of the lungs. The doctor ordered me to stop the tour, suggesting that, if I did not, I might go home in a wooden box. He was afraid that pneumonia would develop. As a result of his warning, I cancelled the remainder of my European tour, aside from a short visit to Rome.

Telegrams were sent to all the co-workers in the countries I couldn't visit, inviting them to come to Basel and receive a tape recording for each of their countries. A public lecture in Basel was cancelled, as was also the one in Locarno, but it was agreed that I would give a private talk to the group of leaders in the two cities.

The following is a report given by Mrs. Zinsstag:

"While George Adamski stayed another week in Basel, Mr. and Mrs. Karl L. Veit, chairmen of the German UFO Study Group, arrived with another staunch supporter, Mrs. M. Muller. They had started a very big organization and advertising campaign in Germany and were desperate when they learned everything had been cancelled. They felt better again when George Adamski generously offered them the right to copy the film so that at least some of the scheduled meetings could be held, though minus George Adamski in person.

"Dora Bauer, liaison worker from Austria, and George Neidhart, Munich organizer, arrived at their earliest convenience. As a compensation, they also got the right to show a copy of the film, as did liaison men Dr. Alberto Perego, of Italy, and H. Petersen of Denmark.

"It cannot be denied that there was another point too, on which G.A. [George Adamski] had his misgivings. UFO study and discussion activities all over the German-speaking part of Europe are very much permeated with Esoteric, Occult and Sectarian concepts. Thus, in these parts George Adamski would not only have had to fight the disbelieving of the so-called Realists, he would also have had to expose himself to the dissent, or even the protests coming from these various factions. Or else, from all appearances, to have accepted the promotion and misplaced protection by innumerable societies, cults, associations, etc."

This ended my European lectures, and I looked forward to a few days rest at Locarno, Switzerland. Basel is located in the northwestern part of Switzerland. To reach Locarno from Basel, I traveled by rail through Zurich, past beautiful lakes and magnificent mountains. The train then rolled on to the southeastern part of Switzerland.

Locarno, in the canton (state) of Ticino, is beautiful beyond description. It is nestled on the slopes of the southern Alps, on Lake Maggoire, near the Italian border. Lovely homes are tucked in among trees and shrubs covering the hills completely around the lake. In the Lake Side Gardens are palm trees such as we have in California. The higher mountains in back of the town were snow-covered. With the sub-tropical trees and flowers in the foreground, it made a beautiful sight.

It was the end of May when I passed through the mountains, and the lovely meadows were aflame with many different species of wild flowers. I was told that many of the rare varieties were protected by law.

Americans I met who live there love the clean, beautiful country.

My stay in Locarno proved a welcome respite from the heavy lecture schedule. The French windows in my hotel room opened to a small balcony. It was peaceful to sit on the balcony in a soft easy chair, to lean back and enjoy the panorama of lake and mountain scenery.

There was time to consider the many events of previous weeks. The true significance of what I had witnessed became clear to me.

For instance: what happened to the money-changers Christ drove out of the temple? It seems as though they have gathered over the centuries in Zurich.

Of course this comparison is allegorical, but the results are apparent.

Zurich, financial center of the world, is the international headquarters for the "Silence Group"! The invisible reins of financial influence extend from Zurich to puppet organizations in every nation! Has it ever occurred to the reader that every nation is financially linked to the Bank of Switzerland, in the country which has enjoyed complete neutrality during every world conflict.

Geneva is a gigantic chessboard where nations of the world are played one against the other, according to the dictates of what the Swiss themselves term "The Colossal Financiers." All of this is accomplished under the cloak of neutrality, in Switzerland, where wars are not permitted to happen!

141

During my tour I had succeeded in alerting too many people to the truth. The overlords cannot tolerate people who think for themselves. That is why suppression of knowledge is necessary to the success of a dictatorship. People who think for themselves are difficult to control, because the minute they realize they are being exploited, they begin to search for truth and freedom.

The only way the "Silence Group" could combat me was to discredit me before the public. If it had not been for the assistance of my friends from other planets, the "Silence Group" would have achieved its aim.

Women are not permitted to vote in some regions of Switzerland. This issue came up for vote while I was there, but the bill was defeated. The reason was clear, now that I have witnessed the "invisible world government" in action; they could not afford to have women "interfere" with their absolute monarchy. It has often been said that "the hand that rocks the cradle controls the destiny of the nation."

In my home country, the U.S.A., women enjoy equal rights—as do the women of other planets—and they have joined their men as equal partners in the journey toward a more harmonious civilization.

I sat on the balcony and thought again of the widespread mysticism that has been falsely applied to the visitors from other planets. The fradulent mystic groups, professing to be in "psychic" contact with the space people, have aided the "Silence Group" immensely. They have caused confusion and kept the entire space program in a state of ridicule.

A public information officer of the United States Air Force once told me that if it had not been for the psychic cultists, the governments could have made their knowledge public long ago. I hope someday the psychics realize they are holding back the very knowledge they desire!

6. END OF THE TOUR

On June 12th, 1959, accompanied by Mrs. Lou Zinsstag, I left Switzerland for Rome, Italy. Her presence proved invaluable, since she could speak and understand both English and Italian and could act as interpreter. Furthermore, she was personally acquainted with both of our co-workers in Rome, neither of whom were too familiar with the English language as spoken by Americans.

At the airport we were met by Dr. Alberto Perego, our first co-worker in Italy, and a group of friends interested in our interplanetary visitors and what they have to teach us. En route from the airport we were driven through old Rome on a portion of the ancient road constructed in 312 B.C., giving us a graphic view of the days when Roman legionnaires marched along this stone-paved thoroughfare.

On account of my health, no lectures were scheduled for me in Italy. This was a pleasure trip which I expected to enjoy to its fullest. I enjoyed too meeting our co-workers and many friends who had written to me through the years. People, I found, are pretty much the same wherever you find them—friendly, kind, generous, with an appreciation of pleasures of many kinds. The greatest dividing line, it seems to me, is the differences in languages which prevents us from being able to thoroughly understand one another.

Rome is a beautiful city, but when I passed through the ancient Colosseum, I seemed to grow sick and cold, for I could sense a reenactment of the days when men were tortured within this great amphitheater. The agonies of those early martyrs seemed to be impressed in the very stones enclosing the arena.

Most of June 13th was occupied in exploration of the ancient structures, and in taking motion pictures of these historic remnants.

The following day a small, private dinner party was given in my honor at the R'storante La Cisterna. The food here was delicious. I was fascinated by the place and its surroundings, the style of clothing worn by the waiters, as well as by their manner of serving. An atmosphere of cordiality and gaiety prevailed which proved both refreshing and relaxing. I enjoyed every moment that we were there, a matter of several hours.

After we had finished eating and were ready to leave, we decided not to call a taxi. After such a large meal, we all agreed that a little exercise would do us good. A very impressive and beautiful sight lay before us in all directions as we walked leisurely down streets brightly lighted by indirect floodlamps, beamed on ancient ruins.

It was midnight when we finally reached a main thoroughfare. Now, we decided, would be a good time to take a taxi; but not one could be found. I was not at all familiar with the streets of Rome, but when my host suggested that we turn in a certain direction, I said, "Oh, no. Taxicana straight ahead." Where such a word for taxi came from, I shall never know. These friends who had so honored me understood little or no English, nevertheless my unexpected comment was a cause for laughter by all.

As we reached the next corner in the direction I had suggested, suddenly, out of nowhere, a taxi pulled up; the driver jumped out, and opened the door. Surprised though we were, we entered. When we gave the name of our hotel, the driver asked, "Americano?"

I answered, "Yes."

Then, instead of driving us directly to the hotel, the driver proceeded to take us on a scenic tour of Rome that lasted until nearly daybreak before he finally drew up before the hotel. Every moment of the trip had been most enjoyable . . . a night I shall never forget! Naturally, we expected to be charged for the extended ride, but the driver refused to accept extra fare money.

"No extra charge," he said. "I am glad to do it for the American."

I have often wondered, since that night in Rome: who was the cab driver? How did he happen to come along at the right moment, in that particular place? How did he recognize me as an American, when so many people have taken me for an Italian, or of Spanish origin?

Although no lectures had been scheduled for me, Dr.

Perego had arranged to speak to a large group of people, including many from the ranks of the military and the church. His talk was excellent, and well received.

I was particularly interested in this meeting, and wanted to personally get the "feel" of the people. For this reason Mrs. Zinsstag, one of my hosts of the dinner party, and I attended, sitting in the back of the auditorium. The speaker, of course, knew that we would be there. So, at the close of his talk, he announced my presence, and asked me to come to the platform that I might answer questions from the audience. I arose, and as I walked down the aisle, people started cheering, and many of those seated along the edge of the aisle reached out to shake my hand. After the unpleasant publicity I had been given and the reactions in Zurich, I was almost overwhelmed by this friendly heartfelt greeting. I shall never forget it.

When the question period was over another ovation began. One priest arose and said, "Thank you, brother, for the information that we have received." Sincere appreciation for my answers was expressed, and for the opportunity to ask questions.

Dr. Francesco Polimeni, the other of our co-workers in Rome, is a professional pressman who has traveled considerably. Much of his lifetime has been spent in seeking the underlying causes behind world events. I enjoyed a short visit in his home, where he and his wife were able to give me a great deal of knowledge regarding unpublished facts that paved the road for conditions as we find them today between nations. Their reports were without emotion or prejudice, of conditions they had personally seen and experienced along with thousands of other people. To me it was most interesting, as well as an added proof of how the people of the world are being kept in ignorance of true conditions by those who know they cannot rule a well-informed public.

All too soon my wonderful vacation in Italy came to an end. I had only visited Rome, but every moment had been filled with interest. I was beginning to feel better, although still not up to my normal strength. On June 17th, 1959, I left Rome by plane for Denmark, where I was to change in Copenhagen for a polar flight to Los Angeles. Captain H.

C. Petersen, our co-worker in Denmark, was unable to get to the airport while I was there, but sent two very friendly and well-informed young men to represent him. Here again I wished there had been more time for me to spend with those friends who did meet me and were so sincerely interested in our interplanetary visitors and the purpose behind their coming.

The polar flight, with its perpetual daylight and monotonous expanses of ice and snow, was another new experience for me. To combat the ice glare, the shades in the passenger lounge were drawn, and we were given blindfolds. In Greenland we made a short refueling stop at a drab, isolated military base.

Winnipeg, Canada, was our next and last refueling stop before arriving in Los Angeles, California. Here I went through final customs. A change of planes here, and I was on my way to San Diego and home, my world tour completed.

Many times since then I have reviewed the events of those six months. I believe the truth was brought to many people of the world, as requested by our space brothers. Yet, to this day I am deeply concerned that the "Silence Group" and other selfish interests might continue to hinder our progress.

One thing is certain: the most powerful instrument in the hands of the "Silence Group" is public apathy! The man who does not care that other friendly humans exist on planets around us is most easily misled by the selfish interests, and unwittingly serves as a tool for the "Silence Group"! Too, those who resent expenditures of public funds for outer space research, preferring vast sums for destructive purposes, are, knowingly or otherwise, contributing to the total destruction of life on this planet.

BOOK III

1. SATAN, MAN OF THE HOUR

Satan, Man of the Hour, was published by me in 1937 as a small brochure. A few minor changes have been made to bring the subject matter up to date and fitting to present day conditions. Lucifer is symbolic of the mortal sense mind.

*　　*　　*　　*　　*　　*

Out in the infinite vistas of space, in the midst of billions of whirling planets and brilliant suns, mere dots in the limitless expanse of the Whole, existed the Presence of Harmony in perfect equilibrium. The Cosmos was at peace throughout its entirety when suddenly some intangible sense of impending disaster seemed to pass through the vastness like a fleeting shadow-form.

A sardonic chuckle slipped out across the ether waves of space, striking an uncanny awe in the heart of every living thing. The calm, lingering movements of the Cosmic clouds changed to a seething, rolling chaos. Earth-planets shook as with a mighty ague. Giant suns became volcanic in their nature and belched forth great masses of fiery vapor. Thunderous vibrations shook the heavens and lightning flashed on a scene of war—a battle of the forces.

Again that taunting laugh reverberated through the Cosmos; and a deep-ringing voice so mighty in its tone that it seemed to dominate and hold in breathless silence all lesser vibrations in the span of Infinity spoke to the Presence of the Most High.

"O God of the mighty cosmos, come forth now and prove your dominion. I, Lucifer, defy your authority; I have usurped your power. I am the greatest force in the universe. You have set your spies upon me and I have deceived them with a mock humility until I should have grown strong enough to openly challenge you. What have you to say, O God? Do you acknowledge me as your superior?"

The incredible stillness that now gripped the body of Infinity seemed, in its very act of insistent calmness, to combat the fiery thunderous voice of defiance. And then, as though proceeding forth on soft fluttering wings of light came the almost inaudible message:

"Lucifer, great archangel, the pride of power within you has blinded you to that Law to which we both are subject—that which exalts itself shall be cast down—and so not I but Law shall answer you. Hereafter you shall be known as Satan. No more shall the mansions of space nor the heavenly hierarchies know your presence. You shall be confined to the regions of Earth. The power you have shall not be taken from you but your field of action shall be limited, for you shall, henceforth, dwell among those Earth children of mine who still are faithful to me. You shall be as one of them until you have learned the meaning of the humility you mocked, and are willing to reunite with me and work as one."

The gentle, fluttering tone vibration ceased, and each atom in space seemed to be held in quiet expectancy. Then, like a tremendous force torn from within the circle of everlasting Cosmic Light, one aspect of that mighty twin infinity shot downward through space. The Law had spoken—Lucifer had become a prisoner of Earth, sentenced by a just decree.

But suddenly this force became a thought vibrating back through the celestial regions with a deep and sinister tone of mockery; "Oh foolish God and god of fools, to trust the loyalty of earthly men. Here shall I reign and teach these children of thine ways of power and self-exaltation!"

* * * * * *

The spring of 1960 dawning upon the scene of economic, political and social dissemination found also the minds of the world inhabitants filled with vague wonderings. The air was filled with talk of strikes, war and want. Every man was deeply concerned with the ever-increasing civil and international complications.

In the lounge-room of a well-known mountain tavern, where innumerable nerve-worn, world-weary individuals retire to seek a few hours' release from the grueling grind of commercial and social activities, sat a group of men, recently engaged in the momentous task of verbally solving the world's problems. A gathering representing in a small way the life of the world: a great captain of industry; a young army officer on leave; a well-known minister whom an adoring congregation had seen fit to release from duty and finance to a much needed rest; a scientist who had stolen away to the alluring peace of this mountain retreat where he might, while working on his latest book, commune with terrestrial nature which he must understand thoroughly in his work with the elements. There was also a jaded bookkeeper from one of the large packing houses, trying in ten short days to absorb enough beauty and freedom and peace to carry him through another year's confinement within an artificially illumined cage.

The hour of midnight was approaching. The great logs in the fireplace crackled and sputtered, but the playing fingers of flame had worked their magic of relaxation, and a lull had come in the conversation. The whistling of a rising wind through the eaves lent an added feeling of security and peace to those well-sheltered individuals who shared the comforts of the tavern lounge.

Suddenly, intruding itself upon their dreamy meditation, came spoken words in tones of supreme compassion; "Poor mortal slaves, shackled and bound by a force they neither know nor understand."

The eyes of the five men turned simultaneously toward the sound of the voice and rested with frank inquiry upon the newcomer who had silently joined them . . . they knew not when. He sat slightly apart, partially obscured in shadow.

"Slaves?" The question was almost as unanimous as the turning of heads had been when the man's voice had first pierced the stillness.

The stranger rose now, leisurely, as though he had absolved time of all responsibility in his life, and strolled toward the open fire where he stood for several moments in silent contemplation, apparently disregarding the question. Yet his very sense of poise and calm assurance seemed to demand, without a tinge of aggression, the unwavering attention of these fellow-beings.

At last he spoke.

149

"I couldn't help overhearing your conversation. You were discussing the interesting question of Who's Who in the world. You had come to no agreement as to the identity of the outstanding Man of the Hour—that dominating figure of the present age whose finger is upon the control switch of the political, social and economic machinery of the world. Shall I tell you who he is—you who are all slaves to him?"

The five men of the world were so taken aback by this abrupt monologue that they neither spoke nor as much as gestured the affirmative answer they would have given.

The stranger's vision rested upon each one in turn—rested not upon the surface of their being, but seemed to penetrate to the very soul of each and draw out of him, as the gaze was withdrawn, the deepest secrets of the individual's life. At last his voice, calm as before, yet carrying a hint of thunder in its tone, jolted them out of their momentary state of lethargy.

"Satan, my friends! Satan is the Man of the Hour!"

The tension was immediately released, and each of the men permitted himself the privilege of a smile. Here, surely, was another religious devotee turned fanatic by a too-intense concentration upon one channel of thought.

"You are a member of the clergy?" ventured the captain of industry.

"No," denied the stranger. "I am merely a student of universal action. I am an observer of Nature's laws and their manifestation in the various degrees of expression."

"Well, whatever you are, you have undoubtedly given us an unexpected answer to the question at hand; but, without the slightest intention of offense, let me say that I do not think many men of today place much belief in that picturesque figure of a somewhat ancient mythology. If you will allow me to lapse into a bit of modern slang, we have given Satan the 'go-by.'"

"And in the meantime old Satan is giving you the 'run-around,'" said the stranger with a quick twinkle of amusement in his eyes. Then, as suddenly turning again to a serious mood, he continued. "Do not misunderstand me, my friends; I am not referring to that much-characterized individual dressed in red tights, with a pitchfork in his hand. I refer to a force—an aggressive force that is predominant in the average human mind today, a force that has become personified in working through so many millions of personal channels. The power of selfishness and greed which Satan represents has become so generally expressed through humankind today that we might easily speak of it as one individual being. The desire for power, personal gratification and self-exaltation, has become so great in man that the human race has practically lost sight of those Cosmic characteristics which compose its inherent birthright. It is struggling and sweating and cursing beneath the whiplash of its Satanic overseer."

Here the widely-famed minister broke in upon the stranger's discourse.

"Don't you think, my friend, that you are putting it a bit too strongly?" he asked. "It is true that the world is in a more or less unsettled condition at the present time, and there seems to be a great deal of evil perpetuated by humankind of today, but that appearance is chiefly due to the fact that the wrongs of man are so generally publicized whereas the right actions are allowed to rest upon their own merits. Do you not think that the religious element of the world can, with God behind it, gain the victory over this Satanic force of which you speak? Right is might, you know."

"But are you sure you know the right?" The stranger looked directly into the eyes of the minister for the space of several moments and then with a slight gesture of dissent, replied, "I suppose you believe yourself to be sincere in what you just expressed. You no doubt consider yourself a true prophet, a messenger of God, but even you, you and thousands of other appointed ministers and teachers of Truth are actually messengers of Satan. You have perverted the laws of the Cosmos even as the so-called criminal element of the world has done. You are teaching not truth but hypocrisy, falsehood and selfishness!

"Nay, save your remonstrances until I have finished." The stranger interrupted his own thoughts to forestall the defense he saw rising in the minister's mind. "Religion, you say, will lead men out of this chaos. Nay, there you are wrong. Even these angels supposedly sent by God to save His children have been perverted by Satan's suggestion of power, fame, wealth and dominance. They have accepted his bribe of

151

earthly acquisitions—serving Heaven but accepting their rewards from Earth. It is these perverted angels who have taught the worship of false gods—gods of revenge and anger. It was religion that withheld the right of free thought, crying 'heresy' to the works of scientific minds such as Copernicus, Galileo, Kepler and hundreds of others; instilling in each new generation those long-cherished prejudices that held their great-grandfathers in slavery to Satan. No, religion as it has been taught and practiced stands only as a symbol of oppression.

"All men are willing to give advice, to preach brotherhood and world unity, but when it comes to living those teachings they are not able to rise above the Satanic thought of self. Thus far will we go and no further, they say. Possession is man's god; greed and selfishness his principle of living. If he continues in the path he now travels, this civilization will destroy itself as others have done."

"No," said the scientist, "we have progressed too far. We are daily unveiling the secrets of life. Science is even now able to do everything except put a soul into form. It can create forms and perpetuate life in those forms. It is true that we have not yet been able to give them intelligence with which to act independently, but we are not through; our research has just begun. We will yet become masters of the elements—masters of life and death. I believe that science will be the savior of this civilization."

"Yes," replied the stranger. "Science has done and is doing much, but even it cannot save these races whose god is temporal power; for, although there are a few men who are working impersonally to benefit the whole of mankind, there are thousands of men who will use the discoveries of those few in the field of perversion. Men are acquiring knowledge but not wisdom. It is one thing to be intelligent; it is another to use intelligence wisely, to control its action. Men today are psychological infants and intellectual giants. The two do not go well together! The marvelous works of science will not forestall mass hysteria which leads to murder and destruction. Science cannot inoculate the entire race against the germ of selfishness as it can against the germ of smallpox. You may learn the secrets of life and death; you may be able to restore the breath to a form, but can you eliminate from that form the fear, the selfishness, the jealousies, envies, greed, hate? Can you instill the sense of absolute brotherhood in the human intellect? No! That is the work of each individual—no one can change the character of a man except that man, himself. He can be taught how to do it, but how shall even this be done when those who guide his moral and psychological progress are themselves dealing in perversions of the Cosmic Laws—separating man's actions into good and evil according to personal judgment?

"Men are too prone to regard our present civilization as a permanent reality. Be not so sure, my friends! Other civilizations have come and gone, and to the All-Intelligence each one is only so great as a wandering speck of dust that appears to the vision of man for one instant as it passes through a fleeting ray of sunshine.

"There were races of highly intelligent men upon this planet at one time. In fact, the first perversion of cosmic principle took place in Lemuria, that great land that existed in the Pacific Ocean, connected with what is now the western coast of the United States. It was an Edenic garden where the inhabitants walked the flowery paths of life in a state of perpetual youth. Human and animal life dwelt side by side without a trace of fear. These men were natural beings. They were so united one with another that they could commune by thought rather than oral expression, and so closely attuned to Nature that they needed not to ferret out the secrets of chemical action but only to use the gifts this planet had to offer. They were what today would be known as great scientists—intuitive scientists. Then gradually Satan began to insinuate strange ideas into the consciousness of those children that had never known any guidance but that of the Great Spirit. He started them on the path of self-exaltation, the path of division. Where at one time they had worked with Nature to produce greater beauty merely as a duty of action toward the Cosmos, they now acted with a thought of reward to self. They engaged in the work of creating objects to please the senses—likes and dislikes were born. They became self-conscious. Each man tried out his power of creation and everything of beauty that each individual conceived was labeled 'mine.' Vanity and possessiveness stole into the sublimity of their Edenic life, and with the thought of 'mine and thine' came greed."

The voice of the stranger seemed to be drifting off, and within the consciousness of each of his listeners arose the living pictures of that ancient land. But now the signs of age seemed to be creeping upon these children of Lemuria—age that eventually led them into knowledge of a mortal death.

Years passed as a flash, hundreds of years, and then the film of memory halted at a scene that shall not easily be forgotten.

A true and humble teacher stood by a group of his fellowmen. His gestures were eloquent of pleading and his words rang out with the vehemence of sincere feeling.

"My children," he was saying, "cannot you see the folly of your ways? Can you not perceive the fact that you are headed for destruction? This land was once a paradise. You were as one happy family sharing the treasures of the Great Spirit's bounty; treasures of peace, of joy, of free expression were yours. You knew no greed, no selfishness, no gross desire for human exaltation. The elements obeyed your command because you governed them unselfishly, recognizing the oneness of all, but now you have lost your holy vision. You have grown to worship those elements that were at one time subject unto you and they have become your master, for that which you worship shall always be greater than yourself. Open your eyes, children of the One Spirit—purge your hearts of this disintegrating force of separation before you totally destroy yourselves and your land. For seven months the earth has been trembling. The elements are rising to mastership. Beware lest they turn against you!"

Even as he spoke, his listeners disrespectfully walked away laughing and chatting. "He has grown old," they said, "and his mind wanders. He cannot understand progress nor realize that the knowledge of our personal creative power is the stimulus that urges us on to greater things."

"Aye," the teacher spoke sorrowfully, "to greater greed, to greater selfishness. I could lead you again to the path of peace but you will not have it so."

And then suddenly upon this unworthy wilderness of

thought, in the midst of this insatiable desire for personal exaltation, the hand of destiny fell. The moving pageant of desire turned to a shrieking chaos as Nature sought a long-due readjustment. The earth shook with a mighty tremor; great chasms appeared in the once-beautiful garden land. Yawning crevasses sucked in their quota of human carnage. The invisible force whipped the ocean waters into a foaming fury and great tidal waves like the tongue of a ravenous beast swept the human creations and the human creators alike into the jaws of abysmal nothingness.

For months the destruction went on, until at last Lemuria was known no more. Only a calm sea and a few of the higher mountain peaks gave tribute to a land that once had been. Then, although no mortal ear could have heard the message that the ethers carried, there rose the sound of victorious yet hollow laughter and the words, "What now, O God of the Universe? You sent your angelic deputy to save these children but he has failed. They destroyed themselves rather than return to you. I, Satan, have been their leader."

But only the insistent solitude, the imperturbable calm of untroubled Consciousness gave answer to the voice, "I will wait, Lucifer, till they come to me of their free will. I will wait."

And so the Satanic force proceeded on. From race to race, from land to land did Lucifer, working through human form, sow dragon's teeth of selfishness, of hate, of pride, of greed that later would destroy all mankind.

There was the highly developed civilization of Atlantea which, like Lemuria, was eventually destroyed. Where Lemuria had turned to the selfish worship of beauty and art, Atlantea became a worshipper of commercialism. Competition was born, and individual enterprises divided men in thought and action.

"What great wizards of commerce we are, what outstanding financiers, what leaders of industry," the people said. "We have builded a civilization that will stand forever."

Then amid the human pride of accomplishment was heard again the voice of a prophet.

"Atlantea, you have gone to an extreme in commercialism; your nation is on the edge of a precipice. You have forgotten your real self; gold is your god. The law of the Cosmos is unity, yet you have divided yourselves, each man against his brother. Can you not perceive that such a state must bring eventual destruction?"

"The words were almost drowned out by a rush of commerce," the stranger said. "The few who heard shook their heads and muttered, one to another, 'He is behind the times, poor man. He does not understand progress. Competition is the power that stimulates greater activity.'

"But Atlantea is gone—eliminated by the hand of Nature."

The voice of the stranger continued on, retouching old threads in the tapestry of memory.

"Egypt, also, was once a promising land, composed as it was of four distinct races of men, bespeaking in that very fact a sense of brotherhood and mutual understanding. It was, in its early days, well-balanced as to material and so-called spiritual expression, but, with its gradual fusion with other races, of which there were at least twelve, religious complications took place. Each race had its individual conception of diety, all of which were expressions of a personal rather than cosmic nature. Eventually all economic, scientific, and commercial activities had to be placed on the shelf while the many people of Egypt fought to the death to uphold their favorite gods and goddesses, of whom there were not less than four hundred and fifty.

"Egypt now rests in the tomb of religious intolerance and superstition.

"The page of memory is turned and now to the sound of clanking steel and the beat of marching feet, to the cries of dying men, through the haze of blood lust and brutal savagery rises the Roman empire—Rome in all the dubious glory of military dictatorship. Above the agonies of human flesh torn by piercing sword and cut by Roman whips rises a voice, calm and compassionate—'As ye would that men should do unto you, do you even unto them.'

"But the ears of the people were deaf, their eyes blind, their hearts turned to stone, and the glory of ancient Rome is but a page in history."

The stranger paused now and studied his listeners for a moment, then continued: "You who are gathered here tonight may well represent our past. The world today is on the brink of a chasm such as none of these civilizations have ever known. All of our past mistakes are summed up in this present age."

He gestured toward the scientist, "We have gone far in mastering the elements; we have gone far in perverting that knowledge. We are inflated with the pride of our creative genius. We have turned the knowledge of chemical action into fields of destruction, using that understanding for selfish purposes. We have mastered the elements, but not ourselves."

His gaze rested upon the industrial leader. "We are slaves to commerce; competition is becoming keener and more underhanded every day. It is becoming merely a case of 'dog eat dog' in the business world. Every man is against his brother.

"And you," he said, pointing to the minister, "you and your order who should be leading men back to the Father represent nothing more than religious divisions and intolerance. You should be a brother to all men.

"Here we have in one group the story of lost civilizations, but what will the men of today profit by the experiences of the past? Will they let those lessons save them from present destruction? Will they as individuals heed the voice of that one true messenger of God who rose above Satan's influence —'Not I but the Father doeth the work. What I see, the Father doeth.' "

"Do you mean to tell us," questioned the scientist, "that what we term progress is wrong; that we should be satisfied with an ox-cart when we can have all of our present modern means of transportation; or that we should turn to the ministrations of a witch doctor when we have so many practical, scientific means of alleviating human suffering?"

"Or that we should tear down our churches and allow the people to become atheists?" broke in the minister.

"Perhaps you would have us close our factories and business houses, do away with our monetary system and revert to the practice of hunting berries for food."

The army officer interrupted the captain of industry. "Yes, and dismiss our armies and navies. What nation do you think would dare do such a thing? Any country as crazy as that would certainly be very quickly torn to bits and devoured by the rest of the world. No, I think that we had better stick to the law of self-preservation by preparedness."

The jaded bookkeeper in a tone of injured meekness put in his word of protest. "You expect men who have spent their time and energy in preparing themselves to perform certain work to give up their jobs to incompetents who have drifted along and exerted no personal effort to attain success in any field of endeavor. Every man has an equal chance. Are we responsible for those who have not the initiative to be outstanding workmen? The best man will always win. Survival of the fittest is Nature's law."

The stranger sat with bowed head, silent before this barrage of protests.

"My friends," he said, "I have allowed you to represent the past mistakes of humankind. You have done it well. The thought of each of you has gone to an extreme in your individual phase of expression, just as the civilizations of the past have done. I could not deny you the right of progress in any field for that would be contrary to Cosmic laws. I only suggest that the progress be turned to a common good instead of individual benefit. I suggest that you do unto others as you would have them do unto you; that you express that feeling of kindness which you now hold prisoner in the stony dungeon of your hearts. And if I take your God from you, I give you in its stead an impersonal Creator that is the same to all men—a Creative Power that knows no good nor evil, right or wrong; the Law of Cause and Effect that says, 'As ye sow ye shall also reap'—the principle of action and reaction that demands or asks nothing of man except a perfect balance in all phases of life."

The soldier rose. "I am afraid, sir, that you are too idealistic for the present age. You will forgive me if I retire?"

The other five rose also and bade the stranger good night.

He sat alone before the dying embers of a once brilliantly flaming fire. "Poor mortal slaves! It is such as these that I would free from bondage."

A sound of laughter floated back to him from the departing men of the world. It bore a taunting quality of derision in its tone.

158

And then silence—calm, imperturbable silence that in its very act of insistent calmness seemed to dissolve the coarseness of all sound and yet to give the impression of a thought —a thought as old as time. "I will wait. I will wait."

2. CONCLUSION

IN CONCLUSION, I sincerely hope this book has answered many of the reader's questions on flying saucers and space people, as well as establishing my own position in this field of exploration.

My preliminary studies, which began with the advent of flying saucers, have now been completed. Of course, this does not mean I intend to abandon the subject, but it does mean that a new program of greater intellectual expansion, along technical and philosophical lines, will be carried out by myself and my associates.

The knowledge shared by our space brothers must now be put to work. I have been advised to proceed in two fields that are vital to our progress—space philosophy and technology—which, we will learn, are inseparable in establishing a peaceful, productive society.

The information conveyed to us must be put to peaceful productive use, that we might in time achieve the same dignified existence enjoyed by men of other planets.

I would like very much to hear from the readers, as to their opinions and personal conclusions on the philosophy and technology contained in this book.

I would also like to convey the thought that from now on, we will be receiving additional data which probably will not be released through official channels—information which will be instrumental in charting the individual's path of progress.

Future studies being planned at the time of this writing include a detailed exploration of man's place in the Cosmos, and his eternal identity as "The Infinite Man."